HUMAN UNDERSTANDING:
Studies in the Philosophy
of David Hume

WADSWORTH STUDIES IN
PHILOSOPHICAL CRITICISM

Alexander Sesonske and Noel Fleming, Editors

HUMAN UNDERSTANDING:
Studies in the Philosophy of David Hume

META-*MEDITATIONS:*
Studies in Descartes

PLATO'S *MENO:*
Text and Criticism

HUMAN UNDERSTANDING:
Studies in the Philosophy of David Hume

edited by
Alexander Sesonske and Noel Fleming
UNIVERSITY OF CALIFORNIA, SANTA BARBARA

Wadsworth Publishing Company, Inc.
BELMONT, CALIFORNIA

WADSWORTH STUDIES IN PHILOSOPHICAL CRITICISM

The idea of a series of Studies in Philosophical Criticism developed in response to a growing problem in American universities. Philosophy can be taught most successfully in small classes; philosophical understanding grows in the course of a dialogue where problems are discussed from diverse points of view by men who differ in experience and temperament. But with the increase in college enrollments, the size of introductory classes has grown larger and the possibility of a dialogue between professor and students more remote. Our hope is that the Studies in Philosophical Criticism will make a dialogue of sorts possible in a class of a hundred, or a thousand, as well as in smaller classes and seminars. Each volume in the series contains a collection of critical writings related to a single classical philosophical text, such as Descartes' *Meditations* or Plato's *Republic*. These critical writings are not substitutes for the classical work, but supplements to it. They should be read in conjunction with the classical text. So used, they will bring to bear on the problems raised by Descartes, Hume, or Plato that diversity of voices and viewpoints which is the heart of the dialogue— and also, we hope, will prompt the student to add his voice to the discussion.

In selecting material for the volumes in the series, the editors have not searched primarily for writings which provide a definitive analysis of the classical text, but have rather selected those papers they thought might be most useful in undergraduate courses in philosophy, both to provoke students into serious engagement with the text and the problems found there, and to present them with a variety of philosophical styles and idioms. Most of the writings reprinted are quite contemporary; they were selected not only for their excellence but also as an indication that many of the classical problems of philosophy persist as centers of current controversy. We believe this format also achieves one prime desideratum: it acquaints the student with both the great works of the philosophical tradition and the most contemporary concepts, techniques, and modes of thought.

CONTENTS

INTRODUCTION
1

H. H. Price
THE PERMANENT SIGNIFICANCE
OF HUME'S PHILOSOPHY
5

Antony Flew
PRIVATE IMAGES AND PUBLIC LANGUAGE
34

Douglas Gasking
CAUSATION AND RECIPES
60

Karl R. Popper
HUME'S EXPLANATION
OF INDUCTIVE INFERENCE
69

P. F. Strawson
THE JUSTIFICATION OF INDUCTION
75

C. D. Broad
HUME'S THEORY OF THE CREDIBILITY
OF MIRACLES
86

Terence Penelhum
HUME ON PERSONAL IDENTITY
99

SUGGESTED FURTHER READINGS
115

HUMAN UNDERSTANDING:
Studies in the Philosophy of David Hume

INTRODUCTION

David Hume has long been famous, or notorious, as the arch sceptic among modern philosophers. Regarded in this way, as he sometimes regarded himself, he might be said to have undermined the whole edifice of human knowledge: first, science and common sense, by his penetrating analysis of causality and induction; second, religion, by his decisive criticism of certain arguments for the existence of God and the truth of religion—e.g., the argument from miracles or the argument from design; third, our sense of reality, by his treatment of the claim that we have knowledge of an external world; and finally, even our sense of ourselves, by his analysis of substance and personal identity. It is no wonder that he awakened Kant from dogmatic slumber.

Closely connected with Hume's scepticism is his empiricism, the doctrine, roughly, that everything we know originates in or is based on sense experience or introspection. He was the last of the great triumvirate of British empiricists; and in many respects a more consistent, rigorous, and thoroughgoing empiricist than his predecessors, Locke and Berkeley, carrying the consequences of the empiricist position far beyond the conclusions they reached. Indeed, the very rigor of Hume's empiricism, with its consequent scepticism, made him a primary target for critics, who claimed that Hume's destructive conclusions showed the inadequacy of an empiricist theory of knowledge. But despite such criticism empiricism has become a dominant philosophical view today, and probably no philosopher of the past is more discussed and more highly regarded than Hume, whose revolutionary views and arguments are now seen as forerunners of much twentieth-century thought.

But to say simply that Hume was a sceptic—or a sceptic whose scepticism followed from his empiricism—hardly does him justice. Hume did not deny or doubt, for example, that events cause other events, or even that all events are caused; rather, he analyzed what is involved in the causal relation and criticized our claim to *know*, or our ability to prove by reason, that the course of nature will continue to be uniform and open to causal explanation. Although Hume did think of himself as a restrained sceptic, his central concern was to carry through a new study of man, which would serve as the foundation of all the sciences. His aim was not to undermine what was otherwise

1

secure, but to show how and why we know what we know and believe what we believe. He sought to understand and analyze those
aspects of human nature and the mind ("human understanding") which
result in knowledge and justified or inevitable belief. And he wanted
to separate such knowledge and belief from beliefs rooted in prejudice
and ignorance.

The articles we have collected in this volume do not cover the
whole range of Hume's philosophy but treat only problems related to
Hume's exploration of the nature and limits of human knowledge. It
is in this area that Hume's brilliance and scepticism have had the
greatest impact, and it is through his theory of knowledge that beginning students are most often introduced to Hume. With one exception all of the problems treated here are discussed in Hume's *Enquiry
Concerning Human Understanding*, the work most widely read as an
introduction to Hume.

We have chosen H. H. Price's "The Permanent Significance of
Hume's Philosophy" to initiate this volume of criticism because it is a
clear and rather broad discussion which considers Hume's accom-
plishments and recognizes some of his shortcomings. After presenting
the major elements in Hume's "empiricist program," Price focuses on
two of the best-known and most influential of Hume's arguments: his
treatment of the notion of necessary connection (a central step in
Hume's analysis of causation), and his discovery of the problem of
induction. Price exhibits the concepts which bothered Hume: *material object, self, cause, necessary connection*; and also notes some of
the Humean terms which should bother us: *idea, image, derived from,
imagination*. The topics treated form the subject matter of most of
the papers which follow.

The second paper, Antony Flew's "Private Images and Public
Language," discusses at length the doctrines that Hume set forth as
fundamental principles in Section II of the *Enquiry*—his distinction between impressions and ideas, and his claim that all ideas are copies of
impressions. These principles are the backbone of Hume's empiricism.
Puzzling questions abound here: What is an idea? Is it an image? If
not, what could it be? If all ideas are images, how are they related to
the words we speak, which ostensibly refer to an external, public
world? If words do not refer to a public world, how can we communicate at all? Hume was not much interested in questions about
words, but Flew argues that just this blinded him to his own untenable
assumptions about language, which led to the great philosophical
errors to be found in his writings.

After setting forth his basic principles, Hume carries out in Sections IV–VII of the *Enquiry* the analyses for which he is most famous, his examination of *causation* and *induction*. Although Hume's views here have already been discussed by H. H. Price, these topics are of such importance in Hume's philosophy that we have included three further papers dealing with them.

Though Hume's name is not mentioned in Douglas Gasking's "Causation and Recipes," Hume's analysis of causation is unmistakably a philosophical ancestor of Gasking's discussion of this concept. Mere "regular succession" will not suffice as an analysis of causation, Gasking argues, as does Hume; but the account Gasking then gives of the circumstances which lead to our saying that one thing caused another is quite different from Hume's. In his attempt to account for our concept of *cause*, Gasking, like Flew, turns to the public world rather than to occurrences in the mind. We might ask whether such a maneuver would have been possible for Hume.

Hume's greatest service to philosophy, it is said, was his discovery of the problem of induction. Hence, we include two articles dealing with this problem. In the first, Karl Popper accepts Hume's refutation of induction, but then severely criticizes the psychological account Hume offers as an explanation of inductive inference and ends by turning Hume's explanation upside down. P. F. Strawson's "The Justification of Induction" is not an overt criticism of Hume but a substantial contemporary treatment of a problem made famous by Hume. Hume concluded that our knowledge of matters of fact beyond the testimony of memory and immediate experience is not based on reason. But this is most disturbing, for it seems to invalidate the most important segments of knowledge, including all of the conclusions of science. Strawson discusses recent attempts to refute or evade Hume's conclusion, and seeks to exhibit the confusion involved in most treatments of the problem.

Hume wrote two notoriously sceptical works on religion—his *Dialogues Concerning Natural Religion,* published posthumously, and the *Essay on Miracles,* published as Section X of the *Enquiry.* C. D. Broad's discussion of the *Essay on Miracles* is a carefully wrought criticism of Hume's conclusion that no human testimony is strong enough to warrant belief in a miracle. What is a miracle? Under what conditions should we be willing to believe that one has occurred? What sort of evidence is relevant? What amount of evidence would be sufficient? Broad's discussion is perhaps as uninflammatory as Hume's was explosive, but it is clear and persuasive and ends on the ironical point of noting that Hume's scepticism about miracles is not really consistent with his scepticism about induction—which perhaps raises a familiar question about the possibility of a consistent scepticism.

Terence Penelhum, in the final paper of our collection, "Hume on Personal Identity," turns us to another famous argument, Hume's discussion of the concepts of *self* and *identity*. When is it proper to call a thing *the same thing?* This is the problem of identity. When the thing in question is a person, the issue is further complicated because we feel uncertain whether a person is a mind, a body, both, or something else. Hume's contention is that change is incompatible with sameness or identity. If a thing changes, it is no longer the *same* thing; we are simply making a mistake if we speak of it as such. Penelhum argues against this contention in the manner of modern linguistic analysis; his article is not only a cogent criticism of Hume but an exhibition of the difference between Hume's method and one contemporary mode of doing philosophy.

The work of Hume most frequently read in introductory classes is *An Enquiry Concerning Human Understanding*. This work is readily available in several inexpensive paperbound editions; a list of such editions is included in the Suggested Further Readings at the end of this volume. Also, almost every collection of readings in philosophy used as a text in introductory courses contains some selections from Hume's *Enquiry*, or his *Treatise of Human Nature*, an earlier work which covers much the same material. Each of the articles in the present volume presupposes some reading of Hume; in selecting them we have assumed that the student will also be reading the *Enquiry*, although most of the articles reprinted here are just as directly related to Hume's *Treatise*. One article, Penelhum's "Hume on Personal Identity," deals with a problem Hume does not discuss in the *Enquiry*. But since the problem itself is of great interest and some editions of the *Enquiry* include the relevant section of the *Treatise*, we have seen fit to include it here.

A. S.
N. F.

THE PERMANENT
SIGNIFICANCE OF HUME'S
PHILOSOPHY*
H. H. Price

I turn first to Hume's formulation of the Empiricist programme. As everyone knows, he formulated it in the dictum "All ideas are derived from impressions." Other people, especially writers on the history of Philosophy, have preferred another formulation: "All knowledge is derived from experience." I think that this second way of stating the programme is much inferior to Hume's own. It is not merely knowledge that is in question, but all the states of mind (including erroneous ones) into which "ideas" enter: belief, disbelief, taking for granted, assuming, supposing—not to speak of volitional and emotional attitudes. Let us look at the matter from the side of language. Take any sentence you like, whether it be a statement or a command or the expression of a wish, and consider any general symbol which occurs in it. (Obviously any sentence must contain at least one general symbol.) Then Hume says: "Show me the impression, the sensible or introspectible datum or set of data, from which your general symbol derives its meaning. If you cannot, I put it to you that your sentence is nonsense, and that you don't know what you are talking about."

Or rather, that is what he is trying to say, but he does not get it quite clear. The word "idea" is one of the most pernicious sources of confusion in the whole history of Philosophy. Among other things, it may mean either a concept or a mental image. Hume was perhaps the cleverest man who ever used the idea-terminology, but even he cannot escape its baneful influence. There are places where he quite explicitly identifies ideas with mental images. But the doctrine that all *mental images* are derived from impressions, whether it is true or false, is not of the faintest philosophical interest. It is a psychological doctrine, not a philosophical one, and it has nothing whatever to do with Empiricism. Empiricism is a theory about concepts, not about images.

* From *Philosophy*, XV (1940), 10–36. Reprinted by permission.

Or, since the word "concept" has a misleadingly subjectivist flavour, let us say instead that it is a theory about our consciousness of universals. It holds that every universal which we are aware of has *either* been abstracted from experienced instances *or* is wholly definable in terms of universals so abstracted. (*Redness* would illustrate the one alternative, *sea-serpentness* the other.)

But perhaps even this formulation of the Empiricist Principle is not wholly adequate. It is, so to speak, too historical. The difficulty lies in the use of the perfect tense, "has been abstracted." There is the same difficulty in Hume's own phrase "derived from," which has a like reference to the past. For how should I set about to test the adequacy of the Principle? I should have to rummage among my memories, and try to recall the sensed or introspected particulars from which I abstracted such and such a universal which I am now aware of. But, obviously, I couldn't recall them in most cases. We are all familiar with the universal *greenness*, but who of us can recall the particulars from which he originally abstracted it? But even if we could recall them, it would not mend the matter. For if this is the right way to test the Empiricist Principle, it follows that the Principle—whether it survives the test or does not—can be nothing but an inductive generalization, like the proposition about the origin of images which I mentioned a few minutes ago; and it too would be a psychological proposition, not a philosophical one.

Let us therefore try to reformulate the Principle yet again. And let us start once more from the side of language, from the consideration of general symbols. First we will divide general symbols into primary and secondary. A secondary general symbol is one which is definable in terms of other general symbols; for example, *murder* is defined in terms of *malice, killing*, and *human being*, and *dragon* is defined in terms of *winged, fire-breathing*, and *reptile*. Eventually, perhaps after a number of stages, we shall come down to certain primary general symbols which cannot be defined in terms of other symbols at all. Now we can restate the Empiricist Principle. It says that the meaning of a primary general symbol is given, and can only be given, by pointing to a particular which we are acquainted with in sense or introspection and saying, "*That* is an instance of what I mean by the symbol 'so-and-so.'" This process of giving the meaning of a general symbol by pointing to an experienced instance is sometimes called *ostensive definition*. So, we may say that since secondary general symbols are reducible to primary ones, *all* our understanding of general symbols, according to Empiricists, rests ultimately on ostensive definition. To put it more vulgarly, the contention is not so much that all our "ideas" are derived from impressions, but rather that they all have to be *cashed* by means of impressions. If any idea is not thus cashable, it is a pseudo-idea; that is to say, the symbol which purports to stand for it does not really stand for anything, though of course this symbol may still be a very useful instrument for arousing emotions in one's hearers or oneself. It is like a forged cheque, which you can't exchange for coin of the realm. We may suspect that there are many such pseudo-ideas which pass current in the world, and that some of them have played no small part both in philosophy and in politics.

This, then, is the Empiricist programme: to show that all ideas are ultimately cashable by impressions, that is, by data which we are acquainted with in sense or introspection, or in any other sort of acquaintance there may be.[1] This programme works admirably up to a point. There are a very great many general symbols whose meaning rests ultimately on ostensive definition. But on the face of it there do appear to be certain ideas, perfectly familiar to all of us, which are *not* thus cashable by reference to impressions. The three which interested Hume most are the ideas of Self, Material Thing, and Cause. The Self is not a datum of introspection (an impression of reflection, in Hume's language); introspection reveals only mental events, not the Ego which is supposed to own them. Again, a material thing is not a datum of sense: it is not a patch of colour, or a sound, or a smell, or a tactual pressure, nor even a series composed of these. And the causal relation is not a sense-given relation, like the relation of sequence within a single specious present, or the relation of right to left within a single visual field. What is Hume to do about these recalcitrant ideas? He must try to show that though they are not themselves directly cashable by reference to impressions, yet they are reducible to others which are so. In the terminology used above, he must try to show that these words are *secondary* symbols (like *murder* or *dragon*): that though they cannot themselves be ostensively defined, they are analysable in terms of other symbols which *can* be ostensively defined. For example, if *cause* is definable in terms of *constant conjunction* and *confident expectation*, *constancy* and *conjunction* might be cashable by reference to sense-experience, *confidence* and *expectation* by reference to introspection.

But Hume also formulates his problem in another way, which is

---

[1] Hume, and most modern Empiricists with him, assumes that there are no other sorts of acquaintance besides these two. It is difficult to see what reasons they can have. Mystical experience, for example, might be—or include—a kind of acquaintance which is neither sensory nor introspective.

in some respects more instructive. He says that he is going to analyse our knowledge of *matters of fact*. The firm and clear distinction he drew between knowledge of matters of fact and other sorts of knowledge is one of his most important services to Philosophy. It is true that once the distinction is drawn, it seems perfectly obvious. But all the great philosophical discoveries are discoveries of the obvious. The great philosopher is the man who first formulates in clear and unmistakable words, and in as general a form as possible, something which has always been hazily familiar to everybody in particular instances. If we say afterwards that he has told us nothing new, that only shows how right he was.

What then does Hume mean by "knowledge of matters of fact"? He uses the phrase in a somewhat technical sense, which requires explanation. His view is this: There are two spheres, and only two, in which certainty in the strict sense is accessible to us. (1) There is the sphere of the sensibly and introspectively evident. There are some facts about present sense-impressions and present introspectible data which are obvious or manifest. When I am acquainted with a red patch, it is obvious or evident to me that it *is* red. (2) There is also the sphere of what Hume calls *relations of ideas*, which includes the truths of Arithmetic, Algebra, and (I suppose) Formal Logic.[2] For instance, we know by this sort of knowledge that $2 + 2 = 4$, or that if A is greater than B, and B is greater than C, then A is greater than C. Hume says very little about knowledge of the relations of ideas, though he fully admits its importance. His view seems to be that such knowledge is *analytic:* e.g., in order to see that $2 + 2 = 4$ you only have to know what the symbols "2," "4," "+," and "=" mean (or, in the other example, what the phrase "greater than" means). Once you do know what they mean, you can see that the denial of "$2 + 2 = 4$" would be a *contradiction.* I say that this seems to be his view; though here as elsewhere he is greatly encumbered by the idea-terminology, and the consequent confusion between concepts and images.

About these two sorts of knowledge—knowledge of the sensibly evident and the analytic knowledge of Pure Mathematics—Hume sees no difficulty. But obviously we *claim* to know a great deal more besides. We claim to know a great many facts about particular material objects, observed and unobserved, and about particular selves; and among these facts there are some which concern necessary connections, as Hume calls them. Whenever we say that A causes B, we are asserting a neces-

---

[2] In the *Inquiry* Hume adds (Euclidean) geometry to the list, though in the *Treatise* he says that it is empirical.

sary connection between them. Nor is this the only case of necessary connection, though it is the most striking. There are also necessary connections in the way of concomitance, for example between the proportion of Natural Kinds: because this is lead, it is therefore heavy and has a low melting point, or because this is iron it is therefore magnetizable.

This kind of knowledge—concerned with selves, material objects, and necessary connections—is what Hume calls knowledge of matters of fact. And he points out that such knowledge (if indeed it deserves the name) is not reducible to either of the other two sorts. Certainly not to knowledge of the relation of ideas. These matter-of-fact propositions are synthetic, not analytic. The cat in the next room is actually a black and white cat. But if it had not been black and white, but yellow or tabby, or, for that matter, green or purple or transparent, there would have been no *contradiction*. As Hume puts it, "the contrary of any matter of fact is still possible." Indeed, if there had been no cat there at all, and no next room, there would have been no contradiction. Again, if water had *not* frozen at 32°F. or if iron had *not* been magnetizable, there would have been no contradiction. The statement that water does not freeze at 32°F. is utterly unlike the sentence "2 + 2 = 5." It is false, but it is not in the least absurd or self-contradictory. These matter-of-fact propositions are what Leibniz called *contingent*. We cannot say that they are true in all possible worlds (as the propositions of Arithmetic are, or of Formal Logic) but only that they happen to be true in this one.

But perhaps our knowledge of matters of fact is somehow reducible to our acquaintance with impressions? It is difficult to see how it can be, though of course it presupposes such acquaintance. Necessary connections, whether of the causal sort or the concomitance sort, are not apprehended by the senses, as colours or sounds are, or again as relations like "above" and "to the right of" are. It might perhaps be thought that material objects are apprehended by sensation. But are they? When I make a statement about an observed material object, I am not *merely* recording certain sense-impressions actually sensed by myself or other people, even though this is part of what I am doing. By "a cat" or any other material-object word or phrase I mean an entity which is a three-dimensional spatial whole, which persists continuously through a long period of time, which remains in being even when observed by no one, which possesses permanent causal properties, and is public to an indefinitely large number of observers. Whereas our sense-impressions are occasional and fragmentary, discontinuous in time, spatially incomplete (for they lack back and insides), and, moreover, it is commonly supposed that each of them is private to the mind which senses it. Thus, though the impressions which I sense might perhaps be constituents of the cat, they cannot possibly be its *sole* constituents. They are altogether too few and too fragmentary. And we think that there are many material objects which are never observed at all. Clearly, *they* cannot be composed of sense-impressions.

Thus in both cases—necessary-connection propositions and material-object propositions—we have what may be called a transcendence of the given. We are not just asserting that such-and-such impressions are or have been sensed. We are extrapolating beyond them.

Lastly, we turn to the third class of matter-of-fact propositions, those about the self. Here the difficulty, as Hume sees it, is rather that we assert something actually *inconsistent* with the given. We attribute to the self an identity which the data of introspection not only fail to warrant, but actually contradict. Our data are a series of diverse psychical events, which "succeed each other with inconceivable rapidity and are in a perpetual flux and movement." When I look into myself as carefully as I can, all I seem to find is that flux of numerically and qualitatively diverse particulars. What reason can there possibly be for saying that I am "the same" person as I was yesterday or last year? Yet each of us does say this, with the utmost confidence.

We may notice in passing that the last two problems—those of material-object propositions and personal-identity propositions—are not so different as they look. In material-object statements, too, we have identification of the diverse, as Hume himself insists. When I come back to my rooms after two hours' absence, I say that the things I now see are "the same" as those I saw before I went out. But the sense-impressions are by no means the same as they were. The ones I sensed two hours earlier are in any case past and gone by now; the ones I sense now are new ones, even if exactly like them. In technical language, they are at least *numerically different* from the old ones. And nearly always they are qualitatively different as well. For instance, the light has altered since I went away, and where I previously saw reds, greens, and browns, I now see nothing but varying shades of grey.

Conversely, though Hume is not so clear about this, statements about the self, no less than statements about material objects, commit us to a transcendence of the given. We think that the self remains in being even when we are not introspecting anything, as in dreamless sleep. Even when we are awake, we think that processes go on in it which we are not introspectively aware of, just as we think that the cupboard has a back and insides which we are not seeing as well as the front which we do see. Moreover—and this he does explicitly point at —we are quite sure that our self has had a continuous existence through a long period of years, even though there are enormous stretches of our history about which we can now remember nothing.[3]

We have now considered two ways in which Hume formulates his problem. On the one hand, he asks what is the source of certain ideas, namely those of material object, self, and necessary connection? What impression do they arise from? (As we saw, he ought rather to have asked what are the impressions by which these ideas are cashed? to what *ostensively definable* symbols can the symbols "material object," "self," and "necessary connection" be reduced?) On the other hand, he asks what is the nature of our knowledge of matters of fact. We can now see that these two formulations are partially equivalent. A matter-of-fact proposition is precisely a proposition into which one or more of these three puzzling ideas enters. Nevertheless, the second formulation of the problem goes farther than the first. For in asking what knowledge of matters of fact is, we are not merely asking for an analysis of certain puzzling ideas; we are also asking what justification we have for using them. Suppose, for instance, that we have given a satisfactory account of what the phrase "necessary connection" *means*, by reducing it somehow to other symbols which are ostensively definable; we have still to inquire what right we have to assert that there are in fact any necessary connections. No doubt in ordinary life, and in science too, people would claim to know that there are many necessary connections. But how seriously are we to take this claim? What the plain man or the plain scientist calls knowledge is perhaps no more than confident belief. Indeed, we are already entitled to suspect that it is no more. For this alleged knowledge is neither sensibly evident, like our knowledge of present impressions, nor yet is it analytic, like our knowledge of the relations of ideas. And if, after all, it *is* only confident belief, we shall have to ask what reasons, if any, we have for it.

We must now consider how Hume solves the problem he has set himself. He has three puzzling ideas on his hands—those of necessary connection, material-thinghood, and personal identity. And he analyses all three by appealing to something which he calls *the imagination*, and more particularly by reference to certain processes which he calls "transitions of the imagination" or "passages of the mind." I am afraid

---

[3] *Treatise*, Book I, part iv, section 6 (Selby-Bigge's edition, p. 262. Everyman edition, pp. 247–248).

I have far too little time to discuss all three analyses in detail. I shall therefore confine myself to the most celebrated of the three, the analysis of Necessary Connection. But I do so with reluctance, even though this is the one to which Hume himself attached most importance. It would be a great mistake to suppose, as perhaps some do, that his discussion of Necessary Connection is his only valuable contribution to Philosophy. On the contrary, his remarks about Personal Identity are not less original and not less penetrating; while the discussion of Material-Thinghood in the section called *Of Scepticism with regard to the Senses*,[4] though it has attracted much less attention than other parts of his work, is in some ways the most brilliant thing he ever wrote.

I turn, then, to Hume's analysis of Necessary Connection. Let me remind you once again that the sort of necessary connection here in question is the *synthetic* sort, as between flame and heat, or between the different observable properties of lead. It is not the analytic or formally certifiable sort, such as we have in the necessary propositions of Arithmetic, Algebra, and Formal Logic. It is not guaranteed by the Law of Contradiction; the denial of it results in no logical inconsistency whatever. If a necessary connection of this synthetic sort is to be established, it must be established somehow or other by observation.

But now the difficulty is that we never *observe* a necessary connection at all. The most we can observe is constant conjunction: whether in the form of repeated sequence, as of heat upon flame or motion upon impact; or in the form of repeated concomitance, as of the visible properties of iron with its magnetizability. Then, where does the idea of necessary connection come from? From what impression is it derived? (Or, as he should have asked, by what impression is it cashed?) Is there perhaps no such impression at all? Yes, Hume replies, there is; but you are looking for it in the wrong place. The right place to look for it is not among the data of *sensation*. You will never find it there; you will only find constant conjunction. The right place to look for it is in the observing mind, among the data of introspection. Suppose you observe the character B accompanying the character A in a number of instances, and never observe an exception. Then, when you observe A again, you will find your mind passing to the expectation of B, its usual attendant. This passage of the mind is something actually felt, though seldom attended to; it is a datum of introspection, or, in Hume's language, an impression of reflection. And it is this felt passage which is the source of the idea of necessary connection. Accordingly,

4 *Treatise*, Book I, part iv, section 2.

Hume says that "necessity exists in the mind, not in objects." All that the "objects" (that is, the data of sensation) have done is to get you into the habit of expecting *B* whenever *A* is presented. "Necessary Connection," then, is not the name of any objective bond, but for a habit of imaginative transition: the felt transitions from the observation of *A* to the expectation of *B*, or even (as we must now add) from the bare thought of *A* to the thought of *B*, its usual attendant. It is what one might call *of-course-ness*. When we say, "this is lead, so of course it is heavy," "when flame occurs, then of course heat occurs as well," the phrase *of course* denotes exactly that felt passage of the mind which Hume is thinking of.[5]

This theory seems at first sight exceedingly paradoxical, as Hume himself predicted that it would. And we are not surprised to find that some people have thought he was denying the existence of necessary connections. But this is a gross error, much like the error of those who think that Berkeley is denying the existence of chairs and tables. If Hume had failed to find any impression from which the idea of necessary connection could be derived (or by which it could be cashed), then certainly he would have been obliged to conclude that the phrase "necessary connection" is a *vox nihili*, standing for nothing at all. And then, if you like, he would have been denying the existence of necessary connections, or, more strictly, he would have been saying that it was nonsense—not even false—to talk about them; though, even so, the analytic or formally certifiable necessitations of Arithmetic and Formal Logic would have remained perfectly intact. But actually he does not fail to find the requisite impression: only he finds it in an unexpected place, among the impressions of reflection (introspection), not among the impressions of sensation.

In short, he is not abolishing Necessary Connection; he is analysing it. The analysis he gives is a peculiar one, certainly, and perhaps it is entirely mistaken. But still it *is* an analysis, and we cannot judge it fairly if we suppose that it is something else.

Let us now consider certain objections to it. First, there is one which he himself discusses.[6] It may be thought that the idea of necessary connection arises from (or rather is cashed by) our own experience of voluntary action, and is then transformed, by some shaky sort of

---

[5] *Treatise*, Book I, part iii, section 14. "Of the idea of necessary connection." Cf. also the parallel discussion in section 7 of the *Inquiry Concerning Human Understanding*.

[6] In the Appendix to the *Treatise* (Selby-Bigge's edition, p. 632) and more fully in section 7 of the *Inquiry Concerning Human Understanding*.

analogy, to the physical world. Do we not observe directly that a volition to move a certain limb *necessitates* the movement of that limb? Or if this is claiming too much, do we not observe that the volition is a *part* of what necessitates the movement of the limb, even if other factors, e.g., processes in the brain, nerves, and muscles, enter in as well?

In spite of all that has been said on this matter since, Hume's own answer seems to be substantially right. Even in this case, he says, you apprehend nothing but constant conjunction. It is only experience, not any kind of direct insight, which tells you what movement will follow what volition. It is true that you may be aware of a feeling of muscular strain or effort—"animal nisus," as he picturesquely calls it in the *Inquiry*. But, after all, this is only a peculiar sort of sense impression; it differs from others in belonging to the sphere of organic or bodily sensation, but it is a sense-impression still. And scrutinize it as you will, you will find no "mysterious bond" between it and the bodily movement which follows it. (Nor will you find any between volition plus muscular strain on the one hand, and bodily movement on the other.) You will only find constant conjunction, together with a tendency to expect that when one of the *conjuncta* occurs, the other will occur as well. And, as a matter of fact, the conjunction is *not* perfectly constant either; it is only exceedingly frequent. There is such a thing as paralysis, when the volition and the effort occur but the expected movement fails to follow.

This answer, I said, seems to me substantially right. Still, there is something which Hume has left out, and until it is dragged into the light of day, his answer leaves us with a feeling of discomfort. There *is* something peculiar about the experience of voluntary movement. That something is not the felt muscular strain, which is sometimes present and sometimes not; many voluntary movements are so easy that we feel no discernible strain or effort in executing them. It is something belonging to another sphere altogether, something epistemological, and in respect of it a man's own volitions do differ from all the other causes or cause-factors which he knows of. A volition is not, so to speak, a mere push of the will. It has an intellectual side; it includes the *entertaining of a proposition*. I am sitting in my chair writing this lecture, and I decide to get up and use the telephone, which is on a table three yards away. This decision of mine includes a piece of thinking, the entertaining of the complex proposition "I get up, walk to the table, and use the telephone." And when I act, I bring into being a series of events which *verify* this proposition. Thus, between the volition and the result there *is* a further relation over and above that of mere sequence in time.

There is a relation of verification. Every voluntary act, or rather every successful one, is among other things the verification of a proposition entertained in the act of making the volition. But although Hume failed to mention this factor in the situation, the omission does not spoil his argument. For *this* relation between volition and result is not the "mysterious bond" which he was searching for and could not find. My entertaining of *p* does not entail the occurrence of events which make *p* true. To suppose that it does is precisely what Freud calls "the fantasy of infantile omnipotence." We merely find by experience that when we will *p* to be verified, the situation does often alter in such a way that *p* *is* verified.

Another and more interesting objection to Hume's analysis of Necessary Connection is this. Suppose that during the year 1937 *B* is repeatedly observed to follow *A*, and never fails to follow it. We shall then form the habit of passing from the observation of *A* to the expectation of *B*, and from the thought of *A* to the thought of *B*. Once the habit has been formed, it will follow from Hume's definition that *A* is the cause of *B*. The two conditions laid down by him have been fulfilled. *A* is constantly conjoined with *B*, and there is a felt passage from *A* to *B* in the mind of observers. But now suppose that in 1938 *A* again occurs repeatedly, but is *not* followed by *B*. The constant conjunction has ceased, the habit of mental transition is broken; and so, according to Hume's definition, *A* does *not* cause *B* any longer. Thus *A* was the cause of *B* in 1937, but in 1938 it was not.

Now, of course, common sense has a simple solution to the difficulty. It says, "You were making a mistake in 1937. You did believe that *A* was the cause of *B*, but really it never caused *B* at all. No doubt they did go together a great many times, but that was just a coincidence."

But Hume himself, it may seem, cannot accept this simple solution. His definition of "cause" obliges him to say that *A* really *did* cause *B* in 1937. For, by hypothesis, there *was* the required constant conjunction, and there *was* the required habit of expectation: and that is all that causation is.

There is a somewhat similar difficulty about *unobserved* causal connections (and unobserved connections of the concomitance sort). We all think that *A* can cause *B*, even though nobody has observed either of them. But if nobody has observed them, the required mental habit can never be set up. And, therefore, although *A* is repeatedly followed by *B*, and never occurs without it, they cannot be causally connected according to Hume's definition of "cause." There is a like difficulty with regard to constant conjunction which you observe but I do not. In relation to you, they will be causal connections (or necessary concomitances, as the case may be); in relation to me they will not. In relation to Sir Isaac Newton, the motions of the moon cause the tide to rise; but in relation to other people, who have not noticed this conjunction and so have not acquired this particular habit of expectation, they will not cause the tide to rise. It is all very well to say as Hume does that "necessity exists in the mind, not in objects." The trouble is that according to him necessity may exist in one mind and not in another.

In short, his account of Necessary Connection seems altogether too subjectivist to be tolerable. It seems that according to him a necessary-connection statement *cannot be mistaken.* For if we have the required feeling of of-course-ness, we do have it; if we haven't, we haven't; and there is no more to be said. And if we have this feeling, we must know that we have it. So, when Jones says that *A* causes *B*, or is necessarily concomitant with it, his statement must be true: unless he is just lying about his own state of mind, in which case the words he utters misrepresent the knowledge which he has. But is it not obvious that people constantly make false causal statements, and make them in good faith?

To all this I think Hume would reply: I admit that these consequences follow my definition, but I do not see any difficulty in them. They only seem paradoxical, he would say, because we start with a twofold prejudice: the prejudice, first, that causality and necessary concomitance are wholly objective relations; and, secondly, the prejudice that causal statements and necessary-concomitance statements are simple, whereas in fact they are complex. Statements about *conjunctions* can be mistaken, and you may easily believe that a certain conjunction is constant when actually it is not. Also, there are doubtless many constant conjunctions which some people have observed and others not, and many more which no one has observed at all. When the plain man insists that there are objective causal sequences which go on regardless of people's feelings and habits, he really only means that there are objective *constant conjunctions;* and here (Hume would say) I thoroughly agree with him. We must, however, remember that every causal statement, and every necessary-concomitance statement, is complex, not simple. Every such statement contains two parts, which must not be confused: an objective part concerning constant conjunctions, and a psychological or introspective part concerning the speaker's habits of expectation. The latter part cannot be mistaken, unless the speaker is just lying about his own feelings. But the former part can be, and frequently is; we very often think that conjunctions are constant when in fact they are not. Again, when we experience the felt passage from an observed event to the expectation of its usual attendant, the expectation to which we pass may very well be mistaken. Nevertheless, we do pass to it; and as we pass, we do feel the feeling of which "necessity" is the name (the feeling of of-course-ness). And in so far as our statement merely says that we feel it, it is perfectly true.

But I think that in spite of this explanation we shall still be dissatisfied with Hume's analysis. We might restate our difficulty as follows: It would appear that if Hume is right, all statements of necessary connection are partly autobiographical. When I say that *A* is necessarily connected with *B*, I shall be telling you something about myself, as when I tell you that I like custard with prunes. But *are* necessary-connection statements autobiographical at all? When I say that flame causes heat or iron is magnetizable, am I talking about myself? Am I revealing to the world a slice of my own mental history? Is this even a part of what I am doing? It seems clear that it is not.

Now, we might try to get Hume out of this difficulty by drawing a distinction which he never draws himself, though he often needs it, in his Ethics not less than his Theory of Knowledge: I mean the distinction between the *autobiographical* and the *expressive*. I will explain it by an example. If I say on a snowy afternoon, "It is an abominably cold day," I am not *saying* that I am disgusted at the weather. If I were, you could appropriately answer, "No, you're not," or, "So am I." On the other hand, neither am I attributing an objective characteristic of abominability to the day, a characteristic additional to its coldness, darkness, etc. What I am doing is to *express* or *give vent to* my feelings of disgust. It is much as if I had said, "It is a very cold day. Boo!"

Now, it might be that statements of necessary connection, though certainly not autobiographical, are nevertheless in part expressive. They may *give vent to* a certain feeling of mine, though they do not *state* that I have it. When I utter the sentence "*A* causes *B*" or "*A* is necessarily concomitant with *B*," all I am *stating* is perhaps that *A* is constantly conjoined with *B;* and perhaps what I am doing over and above this is just to express or give vent to the feeling of of-course-ness which I have when I pass, as I habitually do, from the observation of *A* to the confident expectation of *B*. Thus, it will be true that I am not *talking about* myself; I am only talking about *A* and *B*. But my sentence will also have an expressive function, of expressing or giving vent to the state of mind which I am in.

I think that this revised version of Hume's theory is an improvement, and one which he would himself be ready to accept. It is really quite clear that whatever causal statements may be, they are not pieces of autobiography. Nevertheless, it would not be quite fair to make him say that the word "necessary" functions in exactly the same way as words like "abominable" and "disgusting," which are purely and simply expressions of feeling. The word "necessary," he would hold, is not *merely* expressive of a feeling. It expresses something more complicated. It does give expression to a felt passage of the mind. But we must remember that what we pass *to* is a belief, something which is either true or false. Thus, our causal sentence really does *three* things, not two: (1) it *states* that A has been constantly conjoined with B, which is true or false; (2) further, it *states* that when A occurs again, B will occur again, which is likewise true or false; (3) it *expresses* the comfortable feeling of of-course-ness which we have when we pass, as we habitually do, from the one of these beliefs to the other. Finally, we must notice that the belief to which we pass is not necessarily a *prediction*. Frequently enough it is; having seen many strikings of matches, always followed by flames, I predict that if you strike this match a flame will again follow. But it may be what Mr. Ryle calls a *retrodiction*, as when I infer from marks seen in the snow that a cat has passed that way. And sometimes it is a *juxtadiction* (if I may invent a queer word myself); as when on touching the top of a table in the dark I believe that there are legs now underneath it which I do not feel or see, or on seeing the back of your head I divine the presence of eyes, nose, and mouth now existing on the far side of it.

So much for Hume's analysis of Necessary Connection. What has it done for us? We can see that at least it has completely transformed the question with which we began. We began by supposing that the problem was to analyse a puzzling sort of objective relation (a "mysterious bond" as Hume calls it) somehow subsisting between events or characters *in rerum naturâ*. But it turns out at the end that the only objective relation in the case is constant conjunction. And this conclusion seems unavoidable, once Hume has pointed out to us that the necessary-connection statements in question—causal laws and necessary-concomitance statements—are *synthetic*, and quite different from the *formally-certifiable* statements of necessary connection which we find in Pure Mathematics or Formal Logic.

The problem which we now have on our hands is quite a different one: how, if at all, we can *justify* the transition which we make from observed conjunctions to unobserved ones, the "of-course-ful" transition of which the word "necessary" is the expression? As a matter of psychological fact, we all do make this transition. If we believe that *A* has been conjoined with *B* in many observed instances and has never been observed without it, then we all do proceed to believe that any other *A* you please is also conjoined with *B*. But what *right* have we to make this jump? Given that flame has been constantly conjoined with heat throughout our experience, is this a *reason* for believing that other instances of flame—past, present, or future—are likewise conjoined with heat?

This is the Problem of Induction; and Hume was the first person to see the extraordinary difficulty of it. By what right do we generalize from experience? Have we any right to do it at all? The process of forming an inductive generalization may be regarded as an inference, of which the premise is the observed constant conjunction and the generalization is the conclusion. But what sort of inference is it? The more we reflect on it, the less we like the look of it. This much at least is perfectly obvious—once Hume has pointed it out—that an inference of this kind can never amount to proof. It is utterly unlike the kind of inference which occurs in Pure Mathematics. For, if it were like that, the assertion of the premise (the observed constant conjunction) would be *logically inconsistent* with the denial of the conclusion. But when we generalize from experience, there is no logical inconsistency whatever in admitting the premise and denying the conclusion. If we write *p* for the premise of our inductive inference and *q* for the conclusion, the conjoint assertion *p and not-q* is not a contradiction. Even though flame has been accompanied by heat five million times and never once found without it, it may still perfectly well be false that *all* flames are accompanied by heat. Indeed, the matter is worse than this. It may still be false that *most* flames (more than not) are accompanied by heat. It may even be false that *any* other flame, even one, is accompanied by heat. The hitherto observed conjunction, though frequent and exceptionless, might still be just a very long run of coincidences; anyone who says it is may outrage common sense, but he has broken no rule of Logic. Thus the difficulty is not to show how generalizations from experience can be certain. It is obvious that they can never be, however confident we may feel about them. The difficulty is to show how they can be probable; that is, how they can be *rendered probable by* the evidence of observed conjunctions.

But perhaps it may seem to some of you that Hume is making a fuss about nothing. When we observe an event *E*, you may say we

know beforehand that it must have had *some* cause. It may be very difficult to discover just what the cause was. But, you may say, we also
know beforehand that the cause must lie somewhere or other in the immediately preceding block of events. So we proceed to look for further instances in which *E* occurs. And we find that the block of events
which precedes it is somewhat different in different cases. In this way,
we can hope to *eliminate* all those events which are causally irrelevant
to the occurrence of *E*, until we are left with that one event—it may be
simple or it may be very complex—which *is* the cause of *E*. It is rather
like hunting for the needle in the haystack. You do it by taking away
the haystack, stalk by stalk, until there is nothing left but the needle.

This is the familiar eliminative notion of induction, with its axiom
the Law of Universal Causation. I have stated it in its traditional form,
which still lingers in our textbooks, though in recent times it has been
improved out of all knowledge by such writers as Mr. J. M. Keynes
and Professor Broad.[7] I do not at all want to deny its importance, any
more than Hume himself did (witness the section in the *Treatise* on
Rules by Which to Judge of Causes and Effects).[8] Elimination does
play a very prominent part both in scientific inquiry and in the pre-
scientific inquiries of ordinary daily life. But I want to say, as Hume
himself would, that the eliminative process is secondary, not primary:
subordinate, not fundamental. There are two points to which I would
like to draw attention. The first is that according to the eliminative
conception of it, induction is not really inductive at all. For it contains
no process of generalization. We are supposed to know beforehand that
some one of a certain group of generalizations is true. Our only task
is to discover which one it is. And this we do by disproving all the
members of the group except one. The whole process is just a disjunc-
tive argument, and it is perfectly deductive throughout. It is enabled
to be so, because even one negative instance suffices to *disprove* a universal proposition, although no number of positive instances will prove
it. That is the point of the Baconian maxim *Major est vis instantiae
negativae*.

My second remark concerns the axiom upon which the whole
eliminative procedure is based, the axiom "every event has a cause."
What are we to say of this? Is it self-evident? So far as I can see, Hume
is right in saying that it is not. (We may notice that the advocates of

---

[7] J. M. Keynes, *Treatise on Probability*, part iii. C. D. Broad, *Mind*, 1918
and 1920.
[8] *Treatise*, Book I, part iii, section 15.

Free Will agree with him in this, though they disagree with him in everything else.) The axiom may indeed seem self-evident, because of a terminological muddle. It is possible to use the word "event" in accordance with its derivation from the Latin verb *evenire*, to mean something which "comes out of" something else—a consequence, or a result. And, of course, it is a tautology to say that every *result* has a cause, and "coming out of" is only a metaphor for "being caused by." But we have then to ask, as Hume does, whether it is self-evident that every *beginning of existence* has a cause. Is it self-evident that every beginning of existence *is* an "event" in this queer though etymological sense; that every beginning of existence does "come out of" something else, in the sense of resulting from it? So far as I can see, it is not self-evident. Then is it demonstrable from self-evident premises? I can only say that Hume's refutation of the alleged demonstrations which were current in his own time seems to me absolutely conclusive,[9] and I do not know of any better ones which have been produced since.

But even if this axiom were self-evident or demonstrable, it would not do the trick. In any case, it will only apply to causal inductions. It has nothing whatever to say to inductions concerning concomitances. But even if all inductions were causal, which they are not, this axiom would be insufficient. Eliminative induction is a process of selecting one hypothesis out of a list of hypotheses: you establish one of them by knocking out all its competitors. But you cannot do this unless the list is of *finite* length. If it is infinite, you will get no nearer to establishing your law, no matter how many competitors you knock out. And you must *know*, or at least have reason to believe, that the list is finite. Even this is not enough. The list must be not merely finite, but *manageably* finite; the eliminative process must be one which falls within human capacities. We therefore need a further axiom to limit the number of permissible hypotheses:[10] we have to assume that, given any character C, the number of characters which are *capable* of being necessarily connected with C is finite, and manageably finite. Let us call this assumption the Axiom of Limitation. Will anyone contend that *this* axiom is either self-evident or demonstrable? Perhaps, however, that is asking too much. Perhaps we only require that this axiom should have a finite

---

[9] In the section called *Why a cause is always necessary* (*Treatise*, Book I, part iii, section 3), Hume examines three alleged demonstrations—those of Hobbes, of Locke, and of Clarke—and shows that all three are circular.

[10] The need for this axiom seems to have been first discovered by Mr. Keynes and Professor Broad. I have stated it in my own way, and in a simplified and inaccurate form. Mr. Keynes's name for it is "The Principle of Limited Independent Variety."

probability, not that it should be certain. But is it *self-evident* that it does have a finite probability? I think anyone who says this is self-evident is a very rash man. And anyone who offered to demonstrate it from self-evident premises would be equally rash. If we do attribute a considerable probability to the Axiom of Limitation, at least in some fields of inquiry, the reason surely is that experience supports it. In short, it is itself an induction, reached not by elimination (for elimination presupposes it) but by direct generalization from experience.

But perhaps there may still be some who will deny that Hume's problem is a genuine one. They may say that Hume is pretending to be ignorant of a fundamental fact which he, like everyone else, knows perfectly well: the fact namely that *the Universe is rational*. This, we shall be told, is a necessary presupposition of all our thinking. And what leads Hume into this wilful and almost wicked blindness? Every second-year undergraduate knows the answer: it is the *atomistic* character of his philosophy.

These two contentions, that the universe is rational and that Hume is an atomist, are constantly repeated from one generation to another. They must have great emotive potency, for when we ask what they mean, we find that both of them are sheer muddles. Let us consider them in turn.

If we take it literally, the statement that the universe is rational is plainly false. Only a conscious being can literally be called rational, or irrational either, and the Universe is not a conscious being. Let us suppose, however, that "rational" here means "intelligible." Now, of course, it is obvious that the universe must be intelligible in *one* sense of the word "intelligible"; it must consist of objects which are instances of universals. This certainly is a presupposition of our thinking; for if objects did not instantiate universals, no proposition about any object could be true, or even false. Further, any universe which we can think about must be subject to the laws of Formal Logic. If the universe were such that p and not-p could both be true, then we certainly could not think about it. But what has all this got to do with induction? Absolutely nothing. Every entity in the universe might be an instance of one or more universals, and be subject to the laws of Formal Logic; and yet there might be no laws whatever with regard to the *co*-instantiation of universals—no laws whatever of the form "whenever there is an instance of A-ness there is also an instance of B-ness." And if there were none, the universe could still be thought about, and propositions would be true or false, but induction would be impossible. How can we tell *a priori* that our universe is not like that? We cannot. Indeed, we have good grounds for thinking that in some respects it *is* like that. For instance, there seem to be no rules with regard to the co-instantiation of specific shapes with specific colours: no rules of the form "whatever is cherry-red is also circular," nor, again, of the form "all shrill sounds are followed by acrid smells."

Why, then, has this argument about the intelligibility of the universe appeared so conclusive to so many high-minded persons? Because they have mixed up this wide sense of the word "intelligible" with another and narrower sense, the sense in which it means "orderly" or "systematic." Now if the iniverse is intelligible in *this* sense of the word, then certainly induction is possible. For to say that "*x* is orderly" is just another and more noble-sounding way of saying that it is subject *not* just to the laws of Formal Logic but also to laws of the synthetic sort, laws of sequence or of concomitance: in short, to what we call *natural* laws, the laws which inductive reasoning seeks to establish. But what reason have we for thinking that the universe *is* intelligible in this narrower and more specific sense? That is precisely Hume's problem. And you do not advance one step towards the solution of it by pointing out that the universe is intelligible in the other and wider sense of instantiating universals and being subject to the laws of Formal Logic.

I now turn to the other contention, that Hume errs by being an Atomist. This is an even more extraordinary muddle, and I shall not attempt to unravel it in detail. I will simply ask, what is the positive alternative to Atomism? What do non-atomistic philosophers assert? I suppose they assert that what we are aware of is always a *continuum* of some sort, a continuous stream of events, or of presentations, or what not. Now I am not quite sure that Hume would have denied this, in so far as it is true. (It clearly needs some qualification. On the face of it, there is plenty of *dis*continuity in our experience, as well; for instance, the stream of visual data is interrupted by blinking, and by intervals of sleep and other unconsciousness.) But whether he would have denied this continuity-doctrine or not, it is utterly irrelevant to the problem of induction. Let the world which we experience be as continuous as you please: let it be as continuous as M. Bergson would have it. Let us suppose that in the course of the continuum there are many stretches in which B succeeds upon A. Does this give us the right to conclude that if there is *another* stretch of the continuum which contains A, it will also contain B? Not in the least. Whatever follows upon A will have to follow upon it without a gap or break; nevertheless, it may perfectly well have a different successor each time. And the same applies equally obviously to concomitances. If there are stretches of the continuum where *A* and *B* occur together, the mere fact that it is a continuum does absolutely nothing to ensure that if *A* occurs in *other* (as yet unobserved) stretches, *B* will be there as well. In short, there is no argument whatever from continuity to regularity or lawfulness. The world might be perfectly continuous and yet perfectly lawless—that is, subject *only* to the Laws of Formal Logic. There is no argument either way. The world might be perfectly discontinuous, and yet as lawful as the most ardent Determinist could desire.

Why, then, has the charge of Atomism appeared so damaging? Because the word "atomism" has two quite different senses. An atomist is sometimes a man who denies *continuity;* but sometimes he is a man who denies not continuity but *connectedness.* These two denials are quite different and logically independent. There might be connections (i.e., lawful correlations) between items which were spatially, temporally, and qualitatively discrete. And, in a world in which everything was continuous with everything else, there might be no connections at all. Accordingly, since "atomism" may mean two quite different things, it has two positive opposites, not one. If the "-ism" terminology pleases, we may call them *continuism* on the one hand, *connectivism* on the other. Perhaps Hume did deny continuism. If so, he was wrong: since the world, or some parts of it, does display continuity. But if it is wrong to deny continuism, we cannot conclude that it is also wrong to deny connectivism, or at any rate to be doubtful about it. If "atomism" is equivalent to "anticonnectivism," it is still perfectly open to us to ask, Is not atomism a good thing? What is wrong with it?

I am afraid that these considerations have been tedious. But I hope that I have managed to convince you that the problem of Induction is a genuine one. I must now point out, however, that Hume himself did not see its full extent. There are the following defects in his formulation of it.

(1) He seems to have thought that all generalizations from experience are *universal* propositions—such as, "all flame is accompanied by heat," or "no cows are carnivorous." But this is not true. There are also statistical generalizations, such as "the proportion of male to female births is approximately fifty-two to forty-eight" or "more than fifty per cent of Englishmen have dark hair." It would indeed be queer to describe these as statements of necessary connection; we need some wider phrase such as "reliable correlation." Nevertheless, they are certainly generalizations from experience, and they do raise the problem

of Induction. Nor is it essential that the proportion be numerically formulated. If I say "most trains reach their destination safely," this too is a generalization from experience; and I use it to guide my conduct and to make predictions, though I certainly do not believe that *all* trains reach their destination safely. So, too, with the statement "influenza is sometimes fatal," which despite its purely historical appearance—as if it merely summed up past observations—is in fact intended to apply to hitherto unobserved cases of influenza as well as to past ones. (We can see this if we translate it into the equivalent statement "influenza is a dangerous disease.")

We may notice in passing that this type of generalization does not fall under the Baconian maxim *major est vis instantiae negativae*. The occurrence of even one *A* which is not *B* does disprove the proposition that all *A's* are *B*. But the proposition that a penny falls heads in approximately fifty per cent of cases is not refuted by any finite "run" of tails. And the proposition that eighty-five per cent of swans are white would not be refuted if I found that all the swans in Regent's Park were black.

(2) Hume often seems to think that all inductive generalizations are causal; and those who make it their business to refute him nearly always think so. Certainly, in the *Treatise*, he first introduces the Problem of Induction in a causal context. But it is not true that all inductive generalizations are causal. Some concern concomitances, not sequences. I have already given examples. The most obvious are those concerning the properties of natural kinds, which are of the form "anything which has the properties *A*, *B*, *C* also has the property *D*"; for instance, anything which has the conjunction of visible and tangible properties connoted by the word "iron" also has the property of being magnetizable. This statement does assert a *dependence*, if you like, but the dependence does not involve sequence in time. In the same way, there are many statistical generalizations which concern concomitances, not sequences; e.g., "more than fifty per cent of Englishmen are dark-haired."

(3) The third defect is one I have mentioned already. Hume seems to have thought that an inductive generalization must be either certain or nothing. But, he asked himself, how can they be certain, since it is logically possible for them to be false although the premises (the observation-statements) from which we infer them are true? Now, this is not the right way to put the problem. If we state it in this way, it is obviously insoluble. The right question to ask is how can generalizations from experience have a finite probability, and how can this probability be increased by an increase in the number of favourable

instances? This point may be put in another way, by reference to the reasonableness of beliefs. We should not ask "what right have we to believe inductive generalizations with absolute and complete assurance?" For it is obvious that we have none, as Hume himself has shown. We ought rather to ask "what right have we to rely upon them with some degree of confidence?" We may still have to confess in the end that we have none; but at least the prospect of a favourable answer is more promising.

(4) There is still another defect which I must mention, although it concerns Hume's view of causation rather than his view of induction. He holds that every cause is spatially and temporally contiguous with its effect. Gravitational attraction and the interaction of mind and body are glaring examples to the contrary: for in both we have causation without spatial contiguity. Telepathy is another. Whether there can be causation without temporal contiguity—action at a distance in time—is a more difficult question.[11] Perhaps it would be wrong to call it causation. But why should there not be ultimate and irreducible regularities of sequence where the antecedent event is separated by an interval of time from the consequent, even if you refuse to call them causal? An Empiricist, at any rate, is in no position to rule out this suggestion *a priori*. He may maintain that there are in fact no such non-contiguous regularities, or that they are reducible to regularities of the ordinary kind. But if he does, he is in danger of having to postulate unverifiable entities (e.g., "unconscious" mental events) and this he will not like doing.

It is commonly thought, rightly in my opinion, that Hume's greatest service to Philosophy is his discovery of the Problem of Induction. No doubt, scholars may find that he had been partly anticipated by others; but on this I will only remark, with Professor Whitehead, that "everything has been said before by someone who did not discover it." The defects which I have pointed out in Hume's formulation of the problem can easily be amended, without sacrificing any of his fundamental contentions, and they do not seriously diminish the magnitude of his achievement. If modern logicians have a rather clearer and fuller view of the problem than he had, it is because they stand on his shoulders. A very distinguished authority has recently expressed the suspicion that Hume was "not a great philosopher but only a very clever man." With all respect, I should like to suggest that the dis-

[11] Cf. Mr. Russell on "Mnemic Causation" in *The Analysis of Mind*.

covery of the Problem of Induction is one of the most important advances in the whole history of thought. And if the man who made it is not a great philosopher, I cannot think what philosophical greatness can be.

What solution does Hume offer to the problem which he has discovered? He seems to be in two minds about the matter. Sometimes he holds a purely sceptical view. He then says in effect that the problem is insoluble. It is a psychological fact that we all do make generalizations from experience, and cannot help doing so—as he puts it himself, it is "natural" to make them—but (he says) we have no justification for them whatever; again, we do all feel great confidence in many of these generalizations, but we have no right to feel any at all about any of them. I do not think it would be fair to say that, according to this view, induction is an *irrational* process, in the sense in which the committing of logical fallacies is irrational (or contra-rational, if you like). The contention is rather that it is *non*-rational, like sleeping or breathing, something which falls outside the sphere of rationality altogether. "All our reasonings concerning causes and effects" [he should have said "all our inductive reasonings, whether concerned with causation or not"] "are derived from nothing but custom . . . and belief is more properly an act of the sensitive than of the cogitative part of our nature."[12] And again: "Nature by an absolute and uncontrollable necessity has determined us to judge as well as to breathe and feel,"[13] where the "judgements" in question are predictions or retrodictions based upon inductive generalizations.

But, though Hume is often a sceptic, and always enjoys calling himself one in order to shock his more dogmatic readers, I think there are at least traces in his work of another and more constructive solution of the problem. In this other mood, his view is not so much that induction *has* no justification but rather that it *needs* none. He seems to suggest that it is an autonomous form of thinking, having its own internal standards or norms, which are not reducible without remainder to the rules of deductive inference. We can ask whether a given *piece* of inductive inference accords with these standards, whether it was the right and proper one to make on the evidence which the thinker had before him. But provided that a given piece of inductive inference does accord with the inductive standards, there is no further question to ask. It would be meaningless to ask *again* whether it is a valid inference; you

---

[12] *Treatise*, Selby-Bigge's edition, p. 183; Everyman edition, p. 179.
[13] *Ibid.*

have already discovered that it *is* valid, that is, that it accords with the only standard by which inferences of that type can meaningfully be judged.

I do not say that Hume states his view at all clearly. But certainly he is very far from holding—as a consistent sceptic should—that there is nothing much to choose between science and superstition, good sense and silliness. On the contrary, he is prepared to admit, indeed to insist, that some transitions of the imagination are good and others bad; even though all alike are incapable of being justified by the canons of deductive logic (for in all of them alike the denial of the conclusion is logically consistent with the assertion of the premises), and even though all alike may in some sense be called "natural." There is a remarkable passage in the *Treatise* where he distinguishes between two types of imaginative transition, and two corresponding senses of the word "natural." He says: "I must distinguish in the imagination betwixt the principles which are permanent, irresistible, and universal; such as the customary transition from causes to effects and from effects to causes: and the principles which are changeable, weak, and irregular. . . . The former are the foundation of all our thoughts and reasonings, so that upon their removal human nature must immediately perish and go to ruin. The latter are neither unavoidable to mankind, nor necessary, or so much as useful for the conduct of life; but on the contrary are observed only to take place in weak minds, and being opposite to the other principles of custom and reasoning, may easily be subverted by a due contrast and opposition. For this reason the former are received by philosophy and the latter rejected."[14] (We must notice that the word "philosophy" in Hume's time included what we call "science.") He then proceeds to distinguish the two senses of the word "natural." "One who concludes somebody to be near him, when he hears an articulate voice in the dark, reasons *justly* and naturally; though that conclusion be derived from nothing but custom, which infixes and enlivens the idea of a human creature, on account of his usual conjunction with the present impression. But one, who is tormented he knows not why, with the apprehension of spectres in the dark, may, perhaps, be said to reason, and to reason naturally too: but then it must be in the same sense that a malady is said to be natural."[15]

[14] *Treatise*, first paragraph of Part IV, section 4, "Of the Modern Philosophy" (Selby-Bigge, p. 225; Everyman, pp. 215–16).
[15] S.B., pp. 225–226, E., p. 216. I have italicized the word "justly."

This passage makes it quite clear that Hume is as well aware as anyone of the difference between science and superstition, good sense and silliness. What is the difference? Whether we are scientific or silly, sane or mad, our inductive inferences are none of them demonstrative; the denial of our conclusion, whether it is a sensible or a silly one, is always logically consistent with the assertion of our premises. What, then, *is* the difference? I think it is this. The sensible or sane or scientifically minded man frames his generalizations, and consequently his predictions, retrodictions, and juxtadictions, in accordance with *observed constant conjunctions*. He says "All *A* is accompanied by *B*" only when he has observed a lot of *A's*, and all of them have been accompanied by *B*. The silly or unscientific or superstitious man frames his generalizations and predictions in some *other* way—in accordance with his whims and fancies, hopes and fears, or because he "feels in his bones" that it must be so. He does not look at the barometer or the clouds or the meteorological map before predicting this afternoon's weather. He says it is going to be fine because he wants it to be fine; or, if he is of another temperament, because he has promised to play cricket and would much rather it were wet; or because some man with a loud voice and a big stick told him it would be fine; or because he has consulted the *Sortes Vergilianae* and come upon a passage about the Sun-God Apollo.[16] The one thing he does *not* have regard to is what we call the "lessons of experience." We all behave in this way about some things. But if any one behaved in this way about most things or all things—if he framed his predictions and retrodictions about them without any regard whatever to observed constant conjunctions—then we should class him as a lunatic. I think indeed that it is part of the *definition* of "lunacy" to form one's beliefs without regard to observed constant conjunctions. It is certainly not part of the definition of "lunacy" to be indifferent to the rules of Deductive Inference and other rules of Formal Logic, though no doubt some lunatics do assert mutually inconsistent propositions. For it is notorious that many lunatics are excellent deductive reasoners; the very peculiar propositions that they assert do follow logically from the premises they believe. What makes them lunatics is the nature of their premises. And the

---

[16] In this strange method of prediction, in case any of my readers are unfamiliar with it, one opens the works of Vergil at random and reads the first line on which one's eye falls. There are also *Sortes Biblicae* and, I believe, *Sortes Koranicae*. If civilization breaks down, our successors will no doubt use the *Critique of Pure Reason* in the same way.

objection to their premises is that they are not framed in accordance with the lessons of past experience, but (if Freud is right) in accordance with their own suppressed desires.

To complete this account we need to mention statistical inductions as well as "all or none" generalizations. Suppose we are told that there are a number of swans now residing in the University Parks; and we are asked to bet on the chance that a certain one of them, called *Abraham*, is black. How are we to bet? If you are a sensible man, you will hunt up such facts as the following: that over a long period of years the proportion of white swans to black ones in the Thames Valley has been (say) about ninety-five to five. You then conclude, if this is all the information you have, that the chances of Abraham's being black is small, about one-twentieth, and accordingly you bet against his being so. But now suppose that I on the contrary am silly or unscientific or superstitious. I shall not bother to hunt up statistics, or to recall what ornithologists and other observers of swans have told me. I shall reflect, for example, that "Abraham" is a Non-Aryan name, and I shall conclude that its owner must certainly be black, and bet accordingly. Of course, he may *be* black after all. Nevertheless, my estimate of the chances was silly, even though I happen to win my money: and yours was sensible, even though you happened to lose by it.

Now suppose some philosopher asks us *why* it is sensible or scientific to frame our generalizations and consequently our forecasts in accordance with observed conjunctions. We shall answer that the question is an improper one. To frame them in that way is part of the *definition* of the terms "sensible" and "scientific"; not part of an arbitrary definition of them, invented *ad hoc*, but part of what everyone in fact means by those words. If you ask "*why* is it sensible to generalize and predict in that way," you are really asking "why is it sensible to be sensible" which is a meaningless question: that is, your utterance is not a question at all, though it has the verbal form of one.

You notice that I have carefully refrained from saying that it is *reasonable* to frame our generalizations and predictions in this way. Instead, I have used more humdrum (dare I say "less emotive"?) words such as "sensible" or "scientific." But, you may insist on asking, is induction a reasonable process or isn't it? To this I answer, it all depends on the definition of the term "reasonable." According to one definition of "reasonable," a process of thought is reasonable if it exemplifies the principles of formal or deductive inference, laid down in Formal Logic: and the great exemplar of reasonableness is Pure Mathematics. It is *not* reasonable to assert first p and then q where p and q contradict one another. And it is reasonable to infer r from p if (and only if) p and not-r contradict one another. Now according to *this* definition of "reasonable" inductive inference certainly cannot be called reasonable, since (as Hume pointed out) the denial of the conclusion does not contradict the assertion of the premises. Of course, it cannot exactly be called unreasonable either, for the generalization we assert, or the prediction we make, is *consistent* with the observed conjunctions which are our premises; only it does not logically follow from them. We have to say that an inductive inference is just a series of logically unconnected assertions; in fact, that it is not an inference at all, but just a *non*-reasonable transition from one proposition to another.

Now this was the definition of "reasonable" which prevailed in Hume's time, and it was this that made him a sceptic. For, so long as he was under its influence, he was obliged to say that inductive generalization is natural but *non*-reasonable, as we have just remarked. But it is possible to contend that there is a non-deductive sense of the word "reasonable" side by side with this deductive sense of it. At any rate, as a matter of ordinary English usage there certainly is. In ordinary life, everyone would say that it is *reasonable* to frame your generalizations and your forecasts in accordance with observed past conjunctions, and *unreasonable* to frame them otherwise. The capacity to learn the lessons of experience, to frame one's generalizations (and consequently one's predictions and retrodictions) in accordance with the constant conjunctions which one has observed, and not in accordance with one's whims and fancies, hopes and fears, suppressed desires and the like— this capacity is most certainly an essential element in the make-up of a "reasonable" man, as common sense conceives of him. Thus there is an inductive sense of the word "reasonable" as well as a deductive one. And in everyday usage the word covers the combination of both; if a man is lacking in respect of either, we call him unreasonable, or in extreme cases insane. But I think that, of the two, it is the *inductive* sense which is the more prominent in the ordinary everyday usage of the word.[17]

Now I do not say that Hume himself would accept this solution of the problem. On the whole he inclines more to the sceptical view,

---

[17] This sense of the word "reasonable," as Cardinal Newman hints in his *Grammar of Assent*, corresponds fairly closely to Aristotle's usage of the word φρόνησις (commonly translated, "practical wisdom"). Unfortunately, Newman, like Hume, is obsessed by the purely deductive sense of the word "reasonable," and therefore has to credit the man who makes sensible predictions with a mysterious faculty invented *ad hoc*, which he calls the Illative Sense.

according to which induction is natural but non-reasonable, and there is no more to be said. Still, there are hints in the *Treatise* of the more constructive solution which I have been outlining; and it seems to be presupposed by the *Essay on Miracles*, which is among other things a sketch of the Methodology of History. I have already quoted the passage at the beginning of Part iv, Section 4, of the *Treatise* about the man who hears an articulate voice in the dark and infers to the presence of another human being. Hume tells us that such a man "reasons justly" as well as naturally, although he is reasoning from nothing but a frequently experienced conjunction. Whereas the man who is tormented he knows not why with the apprehension of spectres in the dark does *not* reason justly; *his* reasoning is, so to speak, morbid or abnormal, and is only "natural" in the sense in which a malady is natural. What is this "justness" which is present in the one process of thought and absent from the other? It consists precisely in the fact that the one man infers in accordance with previously observed conjunctions, while the other man does not. Thus Hume is here maintaining that there is another criterion of "just reasoning" over and above the principles of deductive inference enunciated by Formal Logic; he is saying in effect that there is an inductive sense of the word "reasonable" as well as the deductive one.

Now suppose that Hume has stuck to this view throughout his discussion, instead of merely hinting at it in one or two passages. Could he then claim to have solved the Problem of Induction, which he himself discovered? I shall not venture to answer this question. Probably the solution is in any case far too simple, even if adequate as far as it goes. But it does have this much to be said for it, that it solves the problem, so to speak, by *dis*solving it: by suggesting that the problem itself has got something wrong with it, and is really a muddle, arising from an erroneous preconception—the preconception that all valid inference ought to be deductive. Now I think that it is pretty clear that the Problem of Induction *must* somehow be a muddle. Nor is this any disparagement to Hume, who invented it. It takes a man of genius to formulate the fundamental muddles. All the great problems of Logic and Theory of Knowledge are muddles, or puzzles if you like a kinder name; they are not problems in the sense in which we speak of scientific or historical problems, which can be solved by the progress of empirical research. They are dissolved, rather than solved, by dragging to light ambiguities, confusions, and unconscious preconceptions; and further (a thing which goes very closely with this) by inventing a more flexible and less equivocal terminology, in which alternatives can be distinguished which were previously confounded, and others perhaps formulated which were previously overlooked altogether.

Of course, even though the Problem of Induction be a muddle, the solution—or dissolution—of it which Hume advocates in the passages I have referred to is not necessarily the right one. Perhaps it is on the wrong lines altogether. But I should like to say a final word about it, addressed to those who think that the business of Philosophy is to *analyse* the basic convictions of common sense and science, not to establish or refute them: or (what comes to much the same thing) to those who think that the business of Philosophy is to analyse the rules according to which ordinary language functions, not to justify them. Such philosophers—and almost all contemporary empiricists are among them—ought to be favourable to the line of thought which I have sketched; they are obliged by their principles to admit that it goes in the right direction, even if it does not go all the way. For there is no question that in ordinary life we do think that there is an inductive sort of reasonableness ("sensibleness" if you prefer) side by side with and distinct from the deductive sort; and this conviction is certainly embodied in the rules which govern our everyday usage of such words as "reasonable," "intelligent," "sensible," "scientific," on the one hand, and "unreasonable," "silly," "foolish," "insane," on the other.

PRIVATE IMAGES AND
PUBLIC LANGUAGE*

Antony Flew

Section II [of Hume's *Inquiry Concerning Human Understanding*] is a revised, smoother, and more persuasive version of the very first Section of the *Treatise*. These Sections contain the statements of what are often taken to be the fundamental principles of Hume's philosophizing. The method of challenge, which they are designed to explain and justify, is in fact applied here only to the idea of necessary connection; and that application both obscures his fundamental negative insight, and distorts his investigation of the aetiology of the established error. On the other hand, it is to the presuppositions revealed, both in his formulation of the method and in the arguments presented in its support, that we must trace the sources of the two chief grounds for that all-corroding Pyrrhonian doubt which is always threatening to eat away the basis of the sort of world-outlook which Hume is most concerned to defend. Section II is therefore much more important than its brevity might suggest.

Hume is in effect restating in his own way what were at the time the commonplaces of Locke's new way of ideas, supplementing these with one or two precisifying amendments of his own. In the prefatory "Epistle to the Reader" of the *Essay Concerning Human Understanding* Locke himself tells us how his master question arose. Deservedly it is an account almost as well known as Descartes' story of his meditations in the room with a stove. Locke was once one of a party of five or six friends "discoursing on a subject very remote from this" when they "found themselves quickly at a stand, by the difficulties that arose on every side. After we had awhile puzzled ourselves, without coming any nearer a resolution of these doubts that perplexed us, it came into my thoughts that we took a wrong course; and before we set ourselves on enquiries of that nature, it was necessary to examine our own abilities,

* From *Hume's Philosophy of Belief* by Antony Flew (New York: Humanities Press, 1961), pp. 19–50. Reprinted by permission.

and see what objects our understandings were and were not fitted to deal with." The first move in the right direction is to appreciate that our understanding must be limited by the range of ideas available to us. Thus we cannot make progress in physics without acquiring some mathematical and physical concepts. We cannot gain a grasp of politics so long as we remain unfamiliar with such basic political notions as *coup d'état, faction, election, taxation, institution,* or *state.* The next move is to argue that we are not born with any innate ideas: every human mind starts, as it were, "white paper, void of all characters, without any ideas." The third move is to enquire what sorts of ideas we do in fact have, and how these could be acquired from human experience; with the corollary that anyone who talks as if he had some idea which he could not have acquired from his experience must be using words without meaning.

By choosing for his book titles which echo that of Locke's *Essay* Hume suggests that he likewise will be concerned with the nature and limits of human understanding; though he also makes it very clear that he intends to give to his findings a more aggressive employment and a sharper cutting edge than would have appealed to Locke. Now in this second Section he presents his own amended version of Locke's new approach, protesting that really "it requires no nice discernment or metaphysical head" to grasp his meaning.

He, too, advances in three stages. First, "we may divide all the perceptions of the mind into two classes or species, which are distinguished by their different degrees of force and vivacity. The less forcible and lively are commonly denominated *thoughts* or *ideas.* The other species wants a name in our language. . . ." For these Hume suggests the label *impressions.* "By the term *impression* . . . I mean all our more lively perceptions, when we hear, or see, or feel, or love, or hate, or desire, or will. And impressions are distinguished from ideas; which are the less lively perceptions of which we are conscious when we reflect on any of those sensations or movements. . . ."

It might seem that "the thought of man, which not only escapes all human power and authority, but is not even restrained within the limits of nature and reality" is unbounded and unconfined. It might seem that: "What never was thought or heard of may yet be conceived, nor is anything beyond the power of thought except what implies an absolute contradiction." But apparently there is in fact a further limitation; and with this we come to the second stage. For "though our thought seems to possess this unbounded liberty, we shall find upon a nearer examination that it is really confined within very narrow limits, and that this creative power of the mind amounts to no more than the faculty of compounding, transposing, augmenting, or diminishing the materials afforded us by the senses and experience." The analogy which Hume needs here is that of the kaleidoscope, which unfortunately was invented only in the following century. His point is that the imagination is kaleidoscopic, and not genuinely creative; "or, to express myself in philosophical language, all our ideas (or more feeble perceptions) are copies of our impressions (or more lively ones)."

The third stage consists in drawing a methodological moral: "All ideas, especially abstract ones, are naturally faint and obscure . . . they are apt to be confounded with other resembling ideas." Impressions "on the contrary . . . are strong and vivid . . . nor is it easy to fall into any error or mistake with regard to them. When we entertain, therefore, any suspicion that a philosophical term is employed without any meaning or idea . . . we need but enquire, 'From what impression is that supposed idea derived?' " . . .

The first thing to appreciate is that in Hume's official view ideas always just are mental images. Furthermore, the meanings of words are ideas, ideas again being identified with mental images. From time to time, not surprisingly, he says things which are hard or impossible to square with this official position. Nevertheless, there is no doubt that this is his opinion when he is on guard. In the *Treatise* ideas are identified explicitly with mental images on page one: *impressions* are to include "all our sensations, passions, and emotions"; while *ideas* are "the faint images of these in thinking and reasoning."

In the *Inquiry* he is never quite so explicit, but what he does say cannot bear any other interpretation. Thus, he begins this Section: "Everyone will allow that there is a considerable difference between the perceptions of the mind when a man feels the pain of excessive heat . . . and when he afterwards recalls to his memory this sensation, or anticipates it in his imagination. These faculties may mimic or copy the perceptions of the senses, but they can never entirely reach the force or vivacity of the original sentiment." This quotation comes from a discursive and introductory paragraph, and might therefore be discounted. But he insists on the same crucially significant word in his technical formulation: "in philosophical language, all our ideas (or more feeble perceptions) are copies of our impressions (or more lively ones)." "Feeble perceptions" which "mimic or copy" in this way can only be mental images. The identification of meanings with ideas, and hence with mental images, comes out most clearly in the pointing of the methodological moral: when Hume considers that if "we have often employed any term, though without any distinct meaning, we are apt to imagine that it has a determinate idea annexed to it"; or when he entertains the "suspicion that a philosophical term is employed without any meaning or idea."

The upshot is that Hume becomes committed to defending a psychological thesis about the limitations of the capacity to form mental imagery; and to mistaking this for a ground, both for a criterion of the meaningfulness of words, and for a method of clarifying their meanings. Given slight amendment, and considered only as a psychological hypothesis, the thesis is perhaps plausible enough in itself. Yet, as a mere generalization, logically contingent and without any theoretical backing, it could not have the strength to support a challenging criterion of the sort which Hume claims to have supplied. Much more important, such a psychological principle however well supported could have no essential connection with questions about the meanings of words. For the meanings of words are not mental images; the capacity to form mental images is neither a logically necessary nor a logically sufficient condition of understanding the meaning of a term; and to have acquired the concept of something is neither the same thing as, nor even a guarantee of, having learnt to summon up mental images of whatever it may be.

The issues here are as important as they are involved. Hume's position owes much of its appeal to the possibilities of confusing the distinction he was actually making, the proposition which he was in fact maintaining, and the conclusion which he himself wished to rest upon it, with various other distinctions, propositions, and conclusions. Indeed, in expounding his view, Hume employs some phrases and offers some reasons which both suggest and would be more appropriate to other distinctions and propositions. Some of these are not only plausible in themselves but also more suited to support the kind of conclusion he wants than are those to which he is officially committed.

The central mistake of exaggerating enormously the importance of mental imagery possesses the wide and perennial appeal enjoyed by many of the great philosophical errors. . . . It is convenient to begin the work of disentangling some of these knotted issues, and of examining the fundamental mistake and some of its ramifications, by considering the case Hume presents for his proposition that all ideas originate from impressions.

He offers two supporting arguments. "First, when we analyze our thoughts or ideas, however compounded or sublime, we always find that they resolve themselves into such simple ideas as were copied from a precedent feeling or sentiment." This is alleged to apply even in those cases which superficially might appear least amenable to such analysis: thus, "the idea of God, as meaning an infinitely intelligent wise and good Being, arises from reflecting on the operations of our own mind, and augmenting, without limit, those qualities of goodness and wisdom."

The choice of this particular example, which is not that given in the *Treatise,* is interesting. The idea of God is one of the two which Descartes in the fourth Part of the *Discourse on Method* offers as falsifying the counter examples against the maxim: "Nihil est in intellectu quod non prius fuit in sensu." This is the Scholastic ancestor of Hume's thesis that all our ideas are derived from impressions: "the philosophers of the Schools hold it as a maxim that there is nothing in the understanding which has not first of all been in the senses, in which there is certainly, however, no doubt that the ideas of God and of the soul have never been." By urging that this idea can in fact be derived from the internal operations of our minds Hume goes some part of the way to meet the objection that it cannot be constructed out of purely sensory experience. . . .

Descartes also concludes, at the end of the third of his *Meditations,* that: "one certainly ought not to find it strange that God, in creating me, placed this idea within me to be like the mark of the workman imprinted on his work." Hume, by implication, disposes of Descartes' argument for this egregious conclusion when later he comes to urge that it is impossible to know a priori that anything either could not, or must necessarily, be the cause of anything: "If we reason a priori, anything may appear able to produce anything."

In choosing the idea of God as his example to illustrate his first consideration Hume appears momentarily to have forgotten the precise character of the contention which these considerations are advanced to support. For it is peculiarly implausible to suggest that to have this particular concept, that of the God of the theists, is a matter of being able to form some sophisticated construction of mental imagery, however it may have been in the first instance derived. Coming to his second consideration, Hume recovers himself: "If it happen, from a defect of the organ, that a man is not susceptible of any species of sensation, we always find that he is as little susceptible of the correspondent idea. A blind man can form no notion of the colours, a deaf man of sounds. Restore either of them that sense in which he is deficient, by opening this new inlet for his sensations, you also open an inlet for the

ideas, and he finds no difficulty in conceiving these objects." . . .
Similarly, we have to allow "that other beings may possess many senses
of which we can have no conception, because the ideas of them have
never been introduced to us in the only manner by which an idea can
have access to the mind, to wit, by the actual feeling and sensation."

Now, as a piece of armchair psychology, this might, or might not,
be all very well. If Hume had been proposing to leave it at that, it might
also have been all very well to dig in, as he does, against all comers:
"Those who would assert that this position is not universally true, nor
without exception, have only one, and that an easy, method of refuting
it; by producing that idea which in their opinion, is not derived from
this source. It will then be incumbent on us, if we would maintain our
doctrine, to produce the impression (or lively perception) which corresponds to it." This leaves the doctrine a contingent generalization,
open to falsification by the production of a recalcitrant negative instance. But Hume wants also to base a method of challenge on precisely
the same proposition, taking the absence of any appropriate antecedent
impressions as a sufficient reason for saying of any supposed idea that
there really is no such idea: "When we entertain . . . any suspicion that
a philosophical term is employed without any meaning or idea . . . we
need but enquire, 'From what impression is that supposed idea derived?'
And if it be impossible to assign any, this will serve to confirm our
suspicion."

This will not do. It is like announcing that all Jews are good business men, supporting this generalization with some more or less relevant evidence, and then dismissing any suggested falsifying counter
example on the grounds that, no matter what the appearances to the
contrary, the person in question cannot really be a Jew: because,
notoriously, all Jews are good business men; which he is not.

This is an intellectual misdemeanour of a common type, for which
it is salutary to have some easily remembered nickname. Essentially it
consists in: first presenting a generalization as a matter of universal but
contingent fact, something which could without contradiction be
denied (although of course the contention is that it happens to be
true); and then refusing to accept as authentic any counter example
suggested, and this on the sole ground that, as the original generalization is true, what is offered cannot possibly be a genuine case of whatever it is which would falsify it. Since to do this has the effect of changing what started as a contingent generalization into a pretentious
tautology, true in virtue of the conventions for the (mis)use of the
words employed in its expression, the move is sometimes spoken of very

colloquially as going into a *Conventionalist Sulk*. These conventions of misuse really are arbitrary: something which, contrary to common assumption, is not the case with all conventions. Because the metamorphosis is often marked by the insertion of the words *true* or *real* to qualify the subject of the original assertion, the whole operation is also sometimes given various nicknames of the form, *The No-True-Briton (or what have you)-Move*.

These labels apply to what Hume seems to be doing here. It amounts to making such sentences as "all our ideas . . . are copies of our impressions . . ." ambiguous: most of the time they are taken to express a contingent generalization; but at some moments of crisis he apparently construes them as embodying a necessary proposition. Such manoeuvres have the effect of making it look as if the immunity to falsification of a necessary truth had been gloriously combined with the substantial assertiveness of a contingent generalization. But this, as Hume himself is going soon most clearly and unequivocally to insist, is impossible.

The ground which Hume tried to defend is thus manifestly untenable. Yet, to have appreciated that and why this is so is to have reached no more than the end of the beginning. Suppose that someone, ignoring the ill-starred attempt to transmute the original hypothesis into a criterion of meaning, wished simply to test it. Hume confidently announces: "If it happen, from a defect of the organ, that a man is not susceptible of any species of sensation, we always find that he is as little susceptible of the correspondent idea." There is no reason to suppose that he or anyone else in his day had ever conducted a serious investigation, and found that this is in fact so. Indeed the first real investigation to come near this question seems to have been that by Professor Jastrow of Princeton, published in 1888. Jastrow has the priority: unless we are to count Locke's "studious blind man who . . . bragged one day that he now understood what *scarlet* signified," and explained, "It was like the sound of a trumpet," or Hume's own questioning in later life of his friend the blind poet Blacklock. So it looks as if we have here one of those cases, still all too common in the psychological and social field, where a proposition which could be established only, if at all, by close empirical study is strongly held to stand to reason, and to be so obviously true that no systematic enquiry is called for: as when the man on the Clapham omnibus . . . clearly and distinctly conceives that hanging and flogging must be the supremely effective deterrents to murder and to lesser crimes of violence, respectively.

So soon as we begin to consider practically the problems of testing the hypothesis that all our ideas are copies of our impressions a peculiar difficulty emerges. We get in touch with some people who have been totally blind or deaf from birth. We persuade them to visit our laboratory. If it was a matter of assessing the kind of capacity usually studied by experimental psychologists, we should have, or could develop, a suitable battery of tests. It is different with the capacity to form mental images. Hume challenges "those who would assert that this position is not universally true" to refute it "by producing that idea which in their opinion, is not derived from this source." This is radically misleading. It does not even make sense to speak of (literally) producing a mental image. Nothing which could be produced for inspection could count as a mental image. The whole point of calling these *mental* precisely is that they must be (logically) private and not public. In the only (and metaphorical) sense in which it might be possible to speak of producing a mental image for public scrutiny what is involved is the (literal) production not of the image itself but of some description or physical representation.

So there would be nothing for it but to ask our subjects direct questions. Yet how could they understand our questions? No doubt we could explain to the man deaf, but not blind, from birth that auditory images are the auditory analogue of visual images, and that hearing bears the same relation to the ears as sight to the eyes. With the appropriate alterations the same could be done with the blind man. But even if, surprisingly, he did enjoy visual imagery, we surely could not hope for any answers to our questions about its colour. Presumably the only way in which he could ever come to give us what we want would be by first gaining the use of his eyes—by a corneal graft perhaps—and then learning in the usual way which colour words are used to refer to what colours. Then and only then might he be able to tell us that even before his operation he had had vivid green and scarlet imagery, and know what he was talking about when he said so.

This suggests that it may be possible to transpose Hume's psychological hypothesis into something which might possess the power to generate the sort of criterion he wants. Various things he says can be taken as hints. There is a sentence in the *Treatise* which finds no echo in the revised version: "To give a child an idea of scarlet or orange, of sweet or bitter, I present the objects, or, in other words, convey to him these impressions; but proceed not so absurdly as to endeavour to produce the impressions by exciting the ideas." The notion of teaching something to a child has since proved fruitful here; and surely it is just a little curious to be speaking of absurdity, as opposed to error plain and simple, if what is involved is purely a matter of contingent fact. Then, in the first paragraph of the present Section, there is another sentence: "All the colours of poetry, however splendid, can never paint natural objects in such a manner as to make the description be taken for a real landscape." This is incongruous. For in place of "ideas (or more feeble perceptions)" Hume is now talking of something of an altogether different order, descriptions. While in place of impressions (our more lively perceptions) he refers to something else which again is of an altogether different order, a real landscape. For—in spite of his easy insinuation of synonymity, "or, in other words"—physical objects and real landscapes cannot be allocated to the same category as impressions. In the final Section he is able so far to forget his official view of the nature of ideas and of the correct procedure for their clarification as to remark that all difficulty in "those pretended syllogistical reasonings" which occur outside mathematics "proceeds entirely from the undeterminate meaning of words, which is corrected by juster definitions."

One sort of transposition that has been suggested would transform Hume's position, which, if a label is wanted, might be called a psychological imagist empiricism, into a species of logical empiricism. It then becomes the doctrine that the meaning of any word or symbol which we can understand must be explicable in terms of our experience. The crux ceases to be a matter of genetic psychology, of how we have come to have some idea. It becomes instead one of how the meaning of a word is to be understood and explained now. To this such questions as "How would you teach that word to a child?" or "How do we first learn the meaning of that sort of word?" are relevant only, but very importantly, insofar as they help to prise away our illusions. Hume's basic division runs between thinking, in a very broad sense, and feeling, again in a very broad sense. The substitute dichotomy is between language, including the non-verbal varieties, and experience, which amounts to pretty well what Hume meant by *feeling* when he claimed "that it is impossible for us to *think* of anything which we have not antecedently *felt*, either by our external or internal senses."

The original uneasy distinction between simple and complex ideas is replaced by one between indefinable and definable terms. Hume says that complex ideas such as that of God "resolve themselves into such simple ideas as were copied from a precedent feeling or sentiment." The logical empiricist will say that words such as *God*, which are certainly not ostensively explicable (not, that is, explicable by any sort of pointing), are, or must be, definable by means of other words which are, or must be, themselves explicable in terms of actual or possible experience. If in any particular case this cannot be done, he will say that the word in question is one of those "employed without any meaning . . . (as is but too frequent)."

This suggestion we have called a transposition, not a translation, because, whereas the translator represents the original substance in the different words of another language, this replaces it by something substantially different, while nevertheless retaining a certain similarity of structure and theme.

Such a transposition has a great many advantages over its original that started by trying to divide all the "perceptions of the mind" into two classes distinguishable purely by their intrinsic, as opposed to relational, qualities ("their different degrees of force and vivacity"). It proceeded inconsistently to allow that when "the mind be disordered by disease or madness" this may be impossible; while all the time assuming that the proposed division could still be made. It also assumed throughout that the division between ideas and impressions was either the same as or congruent with those between thought and experience, and between language and reality. The transposition avoids these inconsistencies, ambiguities, and false assumptions.

With the original, Hume found he had to admit as an authentic exception to his supposedly universal rule the possibility that someone might form an image of a particular variety within a species of sensation notwithstanding that he had never had actually that particular variety of the sensation. Not allowing this concession to put him off his stride, Hume went on brazenly to dismiss the fault as only a little one: "scarcely worth our observing . . . does not merit that for it alone we should alter our general maxim." The transposition allows us to say that Hume's intuition of irrelevance was at bottom sound here. For the missing shade required could be specified with the help of other colour words. This, after all, is exactly what Hume did when he explained the case he had in mind.

Here one must guard against the temptation to say that some form of logical empiricism was what Hume really meant. It is no compliment either to an author's ingenuousness or to his capacity for self-expression to suggest that he really meant something different from what he actually said. In this case, to follow the promptings of misguided charity would be to make an historical mistake too. The great merit of this transposition precisely is that it replaces by a philosophical thesis what in Hume certainly was, and was intended to be, a psychological proposition. Whatever its offsetting faults, this philosophical thesis is at least of the right kind to support a challenging method of semantic analysis such as he was proposing.

The changes, however, have still not gone far enough. . . . The fundamental thing about mental images is not that they are faint or feeble, lacking in liveliness and vivacity: indeed to some, called *eidetic*, these epithets are inapplicable by definition. The real fundamental is that they are (necessarily) private to the person who has them and (logically) cannot be accessible to public observation in the way in which both material things and such other physical phenomena as flames and rainbows must in principle always be.

The next most fundamental fact is contingent: "It is in the field of imagery that some of the most extreme human individual differences are to be found." This was discovered by Francis Galton, who seems to have been the first person to undertake a genuine and systematic study of imagery. Some of his observations can be philosophically as well as psychologically instructive. To his own great surprise he learnt that "Men who declare themselves entirely deficient in the power of seeing mental pictures can nevertheless give lifelike descriptions of what they have seen, and can otherwise express themselves as if they were gifted with a vivid visual imagination. They can also become painters of the rank of Royal Academicians." Again: "To my astonishment I found that the great majority of men of science to whom I first applied protested that mental imagery was unknown to them, and they looked on me as fanciful and fantastic in supposing that the words *mental imagery* really expressed what I believed everyone supposed them to mean."

The consequences of these two basic propositions should give pause to any philosopher tempted to cast mental imagery for a star role in his analyses. If my having a mental image of a particular sort, or indeed of any sort at all, is to be a necessary condition of the applicability to me of a certain term, then no one else can ever possibly be in a position to know whether or not that term is applicable to me; until and unless, that is, I supply a remarkably uneager world with the supposedly crucial relevant information to which in the first instance I alone have access.

If there was only the necessary truth to take account of, an agile and resolute philosopher might try to escape this consequence by appealing to some presumption of uniformity; which might justify the confident use of the word under discussion, even when no particular enquiry had been made as to the occurrence of the mental imagery specified in his proposed analysis. But in the face of the ascertained brute fact rebutting any such presumption the implication cannot be denied. When the term so analyzed is one which people regularly and unhesitatingly apply to one another without having enquired after the imagery supposedly involved, this would amount to saying that all the positive attributions made were unwarranted, whether or not they happened in fact to be correct. This is surprising: but, since it could be taken as one more indication of deplorably low popular standards of evidence, the paradox might be positively attractive to some philosophers. Another implication, which, in view of the intellectual calibre of so many of those who have little or no image experience, might be felt as more burdensomely paradoxical, is that those who know nothing of mental imagery must all be systematically misusing all the terms to be analyzed in this way. In the face of Galton's discoveries, presumably we just have to accept that this is the case with the expression *mental image* itself, and perhaps one or two others. Neither of these implications alone constitutes a reason anything like sufficient to justify wholesale rejection of such analyses. But both are enough to encourage a cautious approach.

Hume here has comparatively little to say about memory and imagination. Nevertheless, what he does say makes it quite clear that he believed mental imagery to be essentially involved in both. Thus a man's impressions of immediate experience are contrasted with his ideas "when he afterwards recalls to his memory this sensation or anticipates it by his imagination." But suppose we ask how claims to remember may be denied. More light will usually be got from considering what we should have to do to deny an assertion than by wondering what we might say in answer to a request for elucidation.

Someone says: "I remember how that tune went"; or "I can remember the names of all the premiers of the French Fourth Republic"; or "I always remember what Senator McCarthy said about General Marshall." Any of these claims would be denied by insisting: either that the speaker was not in a position to remember any such thing, because he had never been in a position to learn it in the first place; or that he did not in fact know what he said he could remember, because all that he was able to offer in response to a challenge to produce the appropriate information was something less than adequate. Thus, the first claim could be denied either by saying that the speaker had never come across the tune or that he did not know how it went. Again, the second and third could not be maintained in the face of proof: either that the speaker had never been acquainted with the names of the premiers, or with the Senator's words; or that he did not now know those names or those words. It would, however, be entirely beside the point to object to any of the three claims on the ground that the speaker neither was having, nor was able to summon up, any mental imagery from which the information he was claiming to remember might be read off. Since to establish a claim to remember the names of all the premiers of the French Fourth Republic it is sufficient to show that the claimant has at some time in the past been acquainted with the list and that he now knows it, it cannot be the case that all remembering necessarily involves the occurrence of some mental imagery.

The same, perhaps more surprisingly, applies with imagination. There is at least one very common sense of *imagine* in which, usually in a past tense, it is a synonym for *think (probably mistakenly)*: "I had imagined that they were relying on some secret guarantees"; or, to take an example from this very Section, "We are apt to imagine it has a determinate idea annexed to it." Closely connected with this are the uses of *imaginary* and *imagination* in such propositions as "The conspiracy was entirely imaginary"; or "The doctors' plot was a figment of Stalin's imagination." In any of these it would surely be preposterous to reject the assertions simply on the grounds that no mental imagery in fact had or could have occurred.

Then there are the uses of *imaginative* in which people and things are said to be imaginative or unimaginative. To decide which award is more suitable for a particular child it is not necessary first to discover, either directly or indirectly, the quantity and quality of its actual or potential private image life. To say that some piece of architectural design is unimaginative is to say something about the all too public deficiencies of the design, not something about the much more easily tolerated private inadequacies of the images and imaging powers of the architect. It would be a grotesque evasion for some complacent spokesman to pretend to meet the charge without any reference to the building, simply calling in evidence diaries recording the spectacular and varied quality of the logically private life of his protégé.

A third sort of case, and one in which perhaps we come nearest to what philosophers and psychologists usually have in mind when they discuss imagination, is that in which imagining seems at least partly to overlap supposing and conceiving: "Imagine what it would have been like to live under a Nazi occupation, if they had succeeded in conquering Britain too." Yet even here it would surely meet the request in full simply to describe to oneself the consequences of such defeat. Provided your listener did this, and provided he did not seem too unmoved, it would be strange to insist that in addition he must supply himself with a series of grim mental illustrations of those consequences.

There may perhaps be slightly more reluctance to concede this last case. Did not Descartes in a memorable passage at the beginning of the sixth of the *Meditations* urge a distinction between imagining and conceiving? "I remark . . . the difference that exists between the imagination and conception. For example, when I imagine a triangle, I do not conceive it only as a figure comprehended by three lines, but I also apprehend these three lines as present by the power and inward vision of my mind, and this is what I call imagining. But if I desire to think of a chiliagon, I certainly conceive truly that it is a figure composed of a thousand sides, . . . but I cannot in any way imagine the thousand sides of a chiliagon . . ." This presumably is one of the passages from Descartes which Hume has in mind when he entertains, only to reject, the proposition: "What never was seen or heard of, may yet be conceived; nor is anything beyond the power of thought, except what implies an absolute contradiction."

There may also be a similar unwillingness to grant that the occurrence of imagery is not logically essential in some cases of remembering, particularly those in which the suggestion of a presently occurring phenomenon is strongest: "I can remember vividly even now how we watched from our bivouac on the main ridge of the Cuillin while the sun set behind the Western Isles"; or "When he saw the barbed wire all the horrors of Karaganda came back to him."

Nevertheless, the wisest moral to draw from the privacy of mental imagery and from the fact that image experience varies so widely from person to person is surely that we should insist that a reference to such experience is not a necessary part of the meaning of any term, except in those few cases where all or a large part of the point of employing the term lies in its reference to mental imagery. The criterion for whether or not all or a large part of the point lies here is simply whether this reference in fact enters into the actual use. The fact that the differences discovered by Galton lay for so long hidden is a powerful reason for believing that this criterion is rarely satisfied. For if questions about the occurrence of imagery entered into our life and language, as the questions whether he was there and whether the information he is offering is correct most certainly and continually do so enter, then there would be far more direct interrogation and far more unambiguous reporting about mental imagery than there is. In that event the variety of human image experience would surely have been a long and widely known fact. . . . If you never try to make sure before applying a word whether or not imagery has occurred; if you never raise any question about its occurrence when challenging the application of that word by someone else: then the occurrence of mental imagery cannot be an essential part of what you mean by it. Though Descartes' use of *imagination* certainly satisfies our suggested criterion, this is not sufficient reason for saying that in our third case imaging is always even part of what is meant by *imagining*. On the contrary, it was only by specifying and studiously maintaining a distinction between conceiving and imagining that he made his requirement that imaging should occur as an essential working part of his use of the term *imagination*. Where this is not done, imaging is not a logically necessary condition of imagining, in the sense there being given to that word. It seems in fact to be done merely by a handful of philosophers, and by them only when on their very best behaviour.

It is, therefore, clear that imaging is not involved necessarily in all memory and imagination. Applying a similar analysis now to understanding the meaning of a term, it becomes obvious immediately that to say that he understands the meaning of the word *oscillograph*, or that he knows as well as you do what is meant in this context by *election*, is not to make assertions about imagery; although, of course, the particular people concerned may well associate particular images with these words. For, to show that they do not know the meanings, it is enough to show that they do not know how the words are used: that, perhaps, the one thinks that *oscillograph* is a synonym for *orrery;* while the other is under the misapprehension that here to speak of an election is to imply that there will be rival candidates. Nor will it be even relevant to object that someone has no power to form imagery if once it is admitted that he cannot be faulted on his usage. No schoolmaster having satisfied himself that a class had mastered the use of the fresh words he had been teaching them would ever insist on a further examination into their powers of imaging before he was willing to concede that they really had learnt what the terms meant.

Hume's view that memory and imagination both necessarily involve mental imagery does not bear directly on any of the main arguments of this *Inquiry*. But his assumptions, neither argued nor fully expounded, that the meaning of a term is an image, and that understanding the meaning of a term is a matter of having or being able to have the appropriate imagery, are directly though not perhaps ostentatiously relevant. For instance, it is chiefly to them that we must trace the origin of those embarrassing and unresolved difficulties about in-

finite divisibility which are mentioned in the final Section as threats to
the foundations of mathematics; though the branches of mathematics
are the only studies with any really hopeful claim to be "sciences,
properly so called." If this were all, we might treat each of these over-
estimations of the importance of mental imagery as a more or less iso-
lated slip, to be noticed, corrected, and forgotten. But, in fact, they are
all symptoms of an approach to language, and hence to philosophy,
which is wholly inverted. . . .

Unlike such of his classical predecessors as Plato or Hobbes or
Locke or Berkeley, Hume seems himself to have had little interest in
or respect for any questions which he thought of as semantic. Thus,
in this *Inquiry*, he contemptuously presents the upshot of his "recon-
ciling project with regard to the question of liberty and necessity" as a
demonstration "that the whole dispute . . . has been hitherto merely
verbal." The icebergs of his own assumptions about language therefore
make little show above the surface. To appreciate their full enormity it
is best to turn again to Locke, who was very much interested, and who
devoted the whole of the third Book of his *Essay* explicitly to the subject "Of Words." Hume is and always must be the supreme authority
on Hume. Yet, precisely because Hume was not so much interested, it
is Locke's statement which provides the sharper picture of the assumptions Hume inherited.

In the first two chapters of that Book Locke outlines his view.
God designed man to be a social creature, and therefore equipped him
with the capacity "to frame articulate sounds, which we call words."
But this was not enough: parrots could do the same. "It was further
necessary that he should be able to use these sounds as signs of internal
conceptions; and to make them stand as marks for the ideas within his
own mind, whereby they might be made known to others, and the
thoughts of men's minds be conveyed from one to the other." This
notion of the primacy of the private is developed and underlined in the
second chapter. "Man, though he have a great variety of thoughts, and
such from which others as well as himself might receive profit and
delight; yet they are all within his own breast, invisible and hidden from
others, nor can of themselves be made to appear . . . it was necessary
that man should find out some external sensible signs, whereof those
invisible ideas, which his thoughts are made up of, might be made
known to others. . . . The use, then, of words, is to be the sensible
marks of ideas; and the ideas they stand for are their proper and immediate signification. . . . That then which words are the marks of
are the ideas of the speaker: nor can anyone apply them as marks, im-

mediately, to anything but the ideas that he himself hath. . . . But though words, as they are used by men, can properly and immediately signify nothing but the ideas that are in the mind of the speaker; yet in their thoughts they give them secret reference to other things." These other things are, first, "ideas in the minds also of other men" and, second, "the reality of things." (One has all the time to remember that Locke is not making a distinction between ideas and impressions.)

From the premises already stated it follows that these practices are strictly unwarranted. Far from trying to avoid this consequence, Locke, as if gluttonous to outrage common sense, insists upon it. "It is a perverting the use of words, and brings . . . obscurity and confusion into their signification, whenever we make them stand for anything but those ideas we have in our own minds." He remarks next how often words are in fact employed without any accompanying ideas. This he interprets as a lamentable indication of our human propensity to "set . . . thoughts more on words than things." For unless "there is a constant connexion between the sound and the idea, and a designation that the one stands for the other," we are uttering parrot talk: "so much insignificant noise." He even notices: "that no one hath the power to make others have the same ideas in their minds that he has, when they use the same words that he does"; although "common use, by a tacit consent, appropriates certain sounds to certain ideas in all languages," and "unless a man's words excite the same ideas in the hearer which he makes them stand for in speaking, he does not speak intelligibly." Nevertheless, "whatever be the consequence of any man's using of words differently . . . this is certain, their signification, in his use of them is limited to his ideas, and they can be signs of nothing else."

It is worth quoting extensively. Locke's view epitomizes in the sharpest outline one of two very different approaches to language. These set out from opposite directions: the first begins with the logically private realm of one man's experience; the second starts from the common public world of physical things and events, the world of "the reality of things" and of transactions between people. Locke's service is to state quite clearly, emphatically, and unequivocally a position which usually is found operating only as an unnoticed and hence unformulated presupposition; or else, if expressed, is expressed only in a muffled and half-hearted fashion. In this statement he almost seems to go out of his way both to underline some of the paradoxical implications —which leave him unabashed—and to give several hints encouraging an entirely opposite approach.

The main implication is that language is essentially private. It is not, like the ciphers and shorthands in which the cautious Locke himself sometimes wrote, just something which happens to be private only until and unless someone contrives to break into the system. It is that all the words in my language are given their meaning exclusively in terms of my (essentially subjective) experience. Their proper use is always and only to describe that experience and nothing else: "It is a perverting the use of words . . . whenever we make them stand for anything but those ideas we have in our own minds." Experiences, both as ideas and as impressions, are essentially private: "all within his own breast, invisible and hidden from others, nor can of themselves be made to appear." So far Locke is prepared to go himself, most emphatically.

But now, if this is where we have to start, how could it ever be possible by communicating with other people to escape nightmare solitude? If my whole language is applicable to my experience exclusively, and yours is confined equally exclusively to yours, then we can have no common vocabulary at all. No messages can pass between our private worlds. We are even deprived of the consolation of talking extravertedly to ourselves: for it is just a muddle for me to think I can say anything either about the experience of other people or about "the reality of things." At this point, Locke, understandably as well as characteristically, begins to weaken: "It is true, common use, by a tacit consent, appropriates certain sounds to certain ideas . . . which so far limits the signification of that sound that unless a man applies it to the same idea, he does not speak properly." Perhaps after all we can accept Locke's principles while still going on very much as before.

That is not so. For how on these principles could anyone ever be in a position to know that his interlocutor was in fact appropriating the same word to the same idea? Indeed, what sense could he possibly give to the suggestion that someone else had the same, or a different, idea from that which he himself had? If my language were really applicable only to my own experience, to my own ideas (in the Lockean sense), then clearly it must be nonsense for me to speak of the ideas of anyone else. And even if there were any room (which, on Lockean principles, there surely is not) for the concept of directly inspecting an object on display, still it is in the very nature of the case impossible to produce an idea for inspection. Locke expressly insists that there is nothing but an arbitrary connection between particular words and particular ideas: "Words . . . signify only men's peculiar ideas, and that *by a perfect arbitrary imposition* . . . no one hath the power to make others have the same ideas in their minds that he has when they use the same words that he does." Equally expressly he rebukes the assumption that the public use is in any way connected neccesarily with the meaning of a word, with—as he would say—the idea it signifies. Regrettably, "men stand not usually to examine, whether the idea they and those they discourse with have in their minds be the same: but think it enough that they use the word, as they imagine, in the common acceptation . . ."

If there is thus no necessary connection between either the form or the use of the word, the two things which are available to general scrutiny, and the ideas in your mind and in my mind, neither of which can possibly in any suitably literal sense be brought out for public view, then the question remains unanswered, and on Locke's principles un-answerable: "How could I ever know whether the idea I and those I discourse with have in our minds be the same?" There would be no possible way of telling whether your idea of a pineapple was the same as mine, and hence no sense to any distinction between my ideas and your ideas. On these principles, it could make no sense to talk of any-thing but my ideas; and, strictly speaking, it could make no sense even to call them mine. . . .

Interestingly, elsewhere in the *Essay*, Locke shows himself aware of the lack of any possible criterion, though not of the corollary. For he considers, what he presumes to be a logical possibility, "that the same object should produce in several men's minds different ideas at the same time; e.g., if the idea that a violet produced in one man's mind by his eyes were the same that a marigold produced in another man's, and vice versa." It is important to appreciate that the supposition is not of any ordinary, or even extraordinary, form of colour blindness or speech disorder. We are not asked to contemplate: the case of a man who cannot make the colour discriminations which others can, a weak-ness which could be detected by putting him through the Ishihara test; nor yet that of a man whose usage of colour words is manifestly irregu-lar or chaotic, which again is something which everyone could know about. Locke carefully so arranges the specification that there could be no possible way of determining whether his putative supposition was or was not ever realized. He nevertheless suggests that many reasons could be offered for thinking that in fact it is not. Unfortu-nately he excuses himself from offering even one; on the grounds that the question is not relevant to his present purposes, and that anyway it is idle inasmuch as the answer could make no difference to anyone or anything.

This is a remarkable conclusion. On his principles, the possibility of communication depends absolutely on people using the same words for the same ideas in their several minds. Yet here he is arguing: both, exactly as we have done, that on these assumptions there is no way of knowing whether you associate the same ideas with the same words as I do; and, very much as we shall do, that none of this matters because really the crucial thing is the public use of the words. Nevertheless, he still takes it for granted that it makes sense to suggest that, even in circumstances where every conceivable test had been applied and had indicated the opposite conclusion, my idea might be different from your idea.

On Locke's principles, this obviously will not do. For if they were right, he could have no means of giving sense to any talk about other people and their ideas. . . .

So much for the most outrageously paradoxical implications of Locke's approach. Like Hume, he provides also what can be taken as hints towards something entirely opposite. Instead of my trying to start from the essentially private, only to find that I must in consequence be held forever incommunicado in logically private solitary confinement, suppose I begin from the other end, from the public world of "the reality of things" and of transactions between people. In fact, language surely is in the first instance adapted to playing a part in social life. Only very secondarily is it applied to the description or the evocation of logically private worlds. Scarcely ever indeed do any man's imagings become a subject of conversation and of concern to other people.

This contention can be regarded as a weaker version of the extreme Wittgensteinian thesis of the impossibility of any essentially private language. In our perspective, Hume's emphasis on the importance of the Humean ideas of sense is bound to stand out as misplaced, and his whole account of our sensory vocabulary must appear inverted and tortuous. We have already touched on the case he mentions of men lacking the use of one of the standard senses. He also recognizes the possibility of other senses: "It is readily allowed that other beings may possess many senses of which we can have no conception, because the ideas of them have never been introduced to us in the only manner by which an idea can have access to the mind, to wit, by the actual feeling and sensation." The case is one which Locke had already considered. Certainly, it is perfectly conceivable that other beings might possess, or that human beings might acquire, senses that we do not have. But that does not imply that we can have no conception of such senses. If anything, it implies the contrary. It is perfectly possible to know what one of them might be, and to be in a position to test a man's claim to possess that particular possible sense.

Suppose someone claims to have the gift of *Röntgening*, defined as the exercise of a sense bearing to X-rays the same relation as hearing to sounds or smelling to smells. Then the very first thing to do is to experiment to find whether he can detect without apparatus the X-rays which we can only discover indirectly by means of fluorescent screens or Geiger counters or special photographic plates. If he fails this test, then the claim must fall. Even if he passes, there are still one or two more rivers to cross. To enquire exactly how many and what rivers would be interesting. . . . But, for the present purposes, it is enough to add that presumably we should want also to make sure that the candidate sense was localized in some organ, and certainly we should have to satisfy ourselves that it provided a range of experience peculiar to itself and as different from any of the standard ones as olfactory is from visual or visual from auditory.

Now, insofar as Hume's psychological hypothesis is right, what we who lack the gift of Röntgening cannot do is to form any mental image of any quality from this fresh range. Only the man who has the sense can have the appropriate impressions: only the person who has had the impressions can form the ideas. This may very well be true. But it does not even begin to show that we can have no conception of such a new sense. We have in fact just described it. What we shall lack is the new sense. For all the discriminations which might be made by Röntgening we shall need laboriously to employ apparatus, while a whole range of possible sensory experience will be closed to us. This may be a lot to lack, as anyone can appreciate who considers for a moment what the loss of even a minor sense like smell would mean to him. But it should nevertheless be possible to build up a fairly rich Röntgen vocabulary, intelligible both to those who had and to those who lacked the gift of Röntgening.

Certainly there is no theoretical difficulty about giving meaning to words for whatever Röntgen qualities we are able to develop apparatus to discriminate. The fundamental principle is the same which applies to all (public) language: the meaning of a word must be explicable by reference, direct or indirect, to the public world, to "the reality of things." The essense of the operation must be to produce some radiation having and some lacking the quality in question, and with the help of these examples to indicate the class of occasions on which the word is and the class on which it is not applicable. The only difference between pupils relevant in this exercise is that those unable to Röntgen will need apparatus if they are to learn from the examples, whereas those gifted with this sense will not. This one difference, so important perhaps for their lives even if not for their understanding of language, must nevertheless carry with it two linguistic corollaries.

Let us try as far as possible, but without prejudice, to express these in Humean terms. The gifted ones will be able to apply each word they learn to the appropriate variety of impression, and they will also be able to apply it to the corresponding variety of idea if they ever happen to have it. The Röntgen blind cannot apply that word to any impression because, presumably by definition, they cannot have any Röntgen impressions to which to apply it. While even if, incredibly, they did happen to have the corresponding idea, they could not possibly know that the word was applicable. Never having had the impression, they could never have learnt that this was the sort of impression to which the word was applicable, and hence they could have no standard by which to judge that it was also applicable to this idea. Thus it seems that to describe this part of the reality of things, X-rays, it is not necessary to have had any Röntgen impressions, nor yet to have any Röntgen ideas. The impressions are needed only, if at all, in order to enable the person who has had them to describe his ideas; while the ideas themselves are, for the purposes of communication, entirely idle and superfluous.

The question now arises of the function and status of impressions. Consider again a sentence quoted from the *Treatise* earlier: "To give a child an idea of scarlet or orange, of sweet or bitter, I present the objects, or, in other words, convey to him these impressions; but proceed not so absurdly as to endeavour to produce the impressions by exciting the ideas." In our new perspective, the notion of impression also is seen to be redundant. For to understand such words as *scarlet* or *orange, sweet* or *bitter*, and to apply them correctly to the appropriate physical phenomena, it is essential only to know to which things they can and to which things they cannot properly be applied. To be able to do this and to know this it is not theoretically necessary to possess the particular senses of sight and taste. In theory, it is enough to have instruments . . . To possess or to have possessed the particular sense which corresponds is theoretically indispensable merely in the practically trivial and derivative case of the application of the word to one's own mental imagery. Here, though the need to be able to understand the meaning of the word by reference to the public world is the same, instruments cannot substitute for the sense itself; simply because a mental image cannot be produced and presented to them.

Of course, it is perfectly conceivable that a man who had always been blind might not only enjoy visual imagery but might also be able to apply to it the correct colour words. But until and unless he acquired the sense of sight he could never properly claim to know that his private usage had been correct. For the standard of correct usage in any language in which two different people are both to be mutually intelligible and to know that they are, is and can only be a public standard. Terms in such a language may be applicable to (private) images, sensations, and what not. But they can only have and be known to have meaning in these private contexts insofar as that meaning can in one way or another be explained by reference to the public world. So even in this special off-centre case of employing words to describe mental imagery the crucial condition of understanding is not to have enjoyed any sort of necessarily private experience, but to have been able, or to be able, to inspect "the reality of things."

Now it will certainly be objected that this is completely beside the point: either on the ground that to talk of having an impression of "the relish of wine" is just Hume's technical way of describing the agreeable pastime of wine tasting; or on the ground that really impressions are the inescapable intermediaries between us and that reality. The first of these suggestions is both symptomatic of one view of the place of technical terms in philosophy and at the same time unflattering to Hume's achievement as a stylist. It is as an interpretation manifestly mistaken. *Impressions* are defined as constituting with *ideas* the class of "perceptions of the mind." While wine must be (logically) public, the impression of wine, like the idea of wine, must be (logically) private. Whereas the presence of wine tautologically guarantees the presence of wine, the occurrence of an impression of wine is by no means a sufficient condition of the presence of wine—because an impression of wine, but not, of course, real wine, may be hallucinatory. Impressions belong to the category of experiences: wine is cellared in that of physical things.

Hume's own objection would undoubtedly have been urged on grounds of the second sort. Thus, in the *Treatise*, he wrote: "It is universally allowed by philosophers, and is besides pretty obvious of itself, that nothing is ever really present to the mind but its perceptions, or impressions and ideas, and that external objects become known to us only by those perceptions they occasion." This conviction appears in our *Inquiry* as one of two main sources of that extreme Pyrrhonian scepticism which is always threatening to break out of control and "to introduce a universal doubt into all subjects of human knowledge and enquiry." "These are the obvious dictates of reason; and no man who reflects ever doubted that the existences which we consider when we say *this house* and *that tree* are nothing but perceptions in the mind and fleeting copies of other existences which remain uniform and independent."

In one version or another, this basic belief was common ground between Hume and all his major immediate predecessors and contemporaries. . . . The same dogma remains still one of the most widespread metaphysical doctrines, cherished not only by philosophers but also by many others who would repudiate the charge of being in any serious sense metaphysicians. It seems to have an especial appeal for tough-minded working scientists. Nevertheless, however intricate and difficult the task of showing in particular detail what is wrong with even one version and with all the various arguments which might be deployed in its support, it is surely certain that every variety must be wrong. For to express such doctrines at all presupposes the truth of propositions with which they are radically inconsistent.

The arguments developed already against Locke's account of language apply with equal force here too. Humean impressions and ideas are but the twin species of the genus Lockean idea. Working on Hume's own example: if it really were the case that the use of the material thing expressions *this house* and *this tree* is to refer to the perceptions of my mind, then before you could understand what I was talking about when I used the words *tree* and *house* I should have to be able to explain by reference to things to which we both have access what it was that I meant by them. To speak here as Hume does—and in this he is a thoroughly representative spokesman—in the first person plural instead of in the first person singular, or better still quite impersonally, is to the last degree prejudicial and misleading. It takes for granted that it is possible for different people to communicate, while at the same time denying a presupposition of any common language. To understand such a language, and to know that we understand it, we must have access, and know that we have access, to a common public world.

It is only by a systematic failure to launch and to press home a really determined attempt to state the position consistently that its fundamental impossibility is concealed. Consider, for instance, Hume's unblushing use in his account "Of the Origin of Ideas" both of material thing terms and of other terms which quite obviously presuppose a knowledge of material things: "By the term *impression* . . . I mean all our more lively perceptions, when we hear or see. . . ." But to speak of hearing or seeing, as opposed to "hearing" or "seeing," implies that there is something objective and physical there to be heard or seen. And later, in the treatment of the case of the man blind or deaf from birth, he writes: "The case is the same if the object proper for exciting any sensation has never been applied to the organ. A Laplander or a Negro has no notion of the relish of wine." This, no doubt, is all very well in itself. But it is entirely inconsistent with any view that the knowledge of (logically private) ideas and impressions is somehow prior to the knowledge of (necessarily public) material things. For it provides a convincing indication that it is impossible to explain what is meant either by *idea* and *impression,* or by the terms applied to characterize particular ideas and impressions, without immediately or ultimately presupposing both the existence and our knowledge of a public world of physical objects.

The objection which we have been deploying must be distinguished from a similar one often fielded against the same opponents. The other argument starts from the general principle that reality expressions must be logically prior to appearance expressions. *Reality expressions* and *appearance expressions* are simply our own improvised temporary labels for two ad hoc holding categories, each of which brings together an enormous variety of very different sorts of expression. These categories are constructed and these terms introduced solely in order to make one extremely general but nevertheless important point. To understand the meaning of any appearance expression you must already understand the meaning of the corresponding reality expression. To be in a position to say: "It looks to me as if it were a sloth," "Perhaps what the photographs showed were only dummy aircraft," or "They worshipped false Gods"; you must first know what a sloth or an aircraft is, or what a true God would have to be.

From this it is argued that talk about impressions or sense data must be logically secondary to talk about the reality of things. Therefore, all those who have urged that our own sense data, and our knowledge of these sense data, are more fundamental than this public reality, and our knowledge of the universe around us, must be wrong. This misconception is perennially seductive. Philosophers first recognize that it is always conceivable that any material thing assertion may turn out to have been mistaken, and then hope to find in a self-denying confinement to some sort of appearance proposition a security against this endemic possibility of error. The temptation is to think that, since the way to be cautious and to minimize your assertive commitments in any one particular case is to confine yourself to appearance assertions, and to eschew all reckless statements as to what actually is, the whole terminology of appearance must therefore be somehow more basic and elementary than that of unhesitating and categorical commitment about reality. This is exactly the reverse of the truth.

The second objection, appealing to the priority of the category of reality over that of appearance, is in that respect similar to the first; which appeals to the priority of the necessarily public over the logically private; and which insists on the knowledge of a common world as a presupposition of mutual intelligibility. Its basis is certainly sound, although excessively difficult to formulate satisfactorily. For it surely is hopeless to try to analyze the meaning of a reality expression such as *That is a kipper* in terms only of appearance expressions: whether categorical, like *It looks to me like a kipper;* or merely hypothetical, like *It would look like a kipper to you if you were here.* This should occasion no surprise. A large part of the point of having these important sorts of appearance expression precisely is to enable us to make guarded statements, without thereby committing ourselves to asserting outright that things in themselves do actually stand thus and thus.

Nevertheless, the second objection, unlike the first, contains a fatal flaw. For it assumes a false equation between appearance talk and talk about the private impressions or sense data of the speaker. Unless this assumption is made the objection is not even relevant: for it is concerned with the priority of reality over appearance expressions: while the supposed opponent speaks only of his own impressions and sense data. But the equation is false. For talk about how things look and about what they appear to be is either forthright talk about the looks of things or else guarded talk about how things are. Whereas discourse about my private impressions and sense data would be wholly autobiographical, and not necessarily either superficial or guarded. If I claim that a figure looks square, then the appropriate verification procedure is either to look to see if it does or else to measure the sides and the angles to discover whether it really is. It would be entirely beside the point to ask me to introspect more carefully.

Our everyday vocabulary equips us richly to make a wide range of subtly different assertions, both forthright and guarded, about both things and the looks of things. (This is a fact which is inevitably concealed by our present use of the wholesale category *appearance expression.*) But it is only by a special effort that we can make clear what we are up to if for some reason we want to describe neither things as they are, nor yet the public appearances of things, but rather and exclusively our private impressions and sense data.

CAUSATION AND RECIPES*

Douglas Gasking

We sometimes speak of one thing, or of one sort of thing, causing another—of the second as being the result of or due to the former. In what
circumstances do we do so?

If we start with some typical statements of causal connection—
"The train-smash was due to a buckled rail"; "Vitamin B deficiency
causes beri-beri"—two things are likely to strike us. First, the effect is
something that comes into being after the cause, and secondly, we suppose that anyone fully conversant with the circumstances and the
relevant causal laws could, from a knowledge of the cause, predict the
effect. So it is very natural to suggest, as an answer to our question:
We say that A causes B whenever a person with the requisite empirical
information could infer from the occurrence of A to the subsequent
occurrence of B. Or we might put it: We say that A causes B whenever
B regularly follows A.

But this "regular succession" notion will not do. For there are
cases where we would speak of A causing B where it is not the case
that from the occurrence of A we may infer the subsequent occurrence
of B.

An example to illustrate this: Iron begins to glow when its temperature reaches a certain point. I do not know what that temperature
is: for the sake of the illustration I will suppose it to be 1,000°C., and
will assume that iron never glows except at or above this temperature.
Now, if someone saw a bar of iron glowing and, being quite ignorant
of the physical facts, asked: "What makes that iron glow? What causes
it to glow?" we should answer: "It is glowing because it is at a temperature of 1,000°C. or more." The glowing, B, is caused by the high
temperature, A. And here the B that is caused is not an event subsequent
to the cause A. Iron reaches 1,000°C. and begins glowing at the same
instant. Another example: Current from a battery is flowing through a
variable resistance, and we have a voltmeter connected to the two poles
of the battery to measure the potential difference. Its reading is steady.

* From *Mind*, LXIV (1955), 479–487. Reprinted by permission.

We now turn the knob of our variable resistance and immediately the voltmeter shows that the potential difference has increased. If someone now asks: "What caused this increase?" we reply: "The increase of the resistance in the circuit." But here again the effect was not something subsequent to the cause, but simultaneous.

So perhaps our account should be emended so as to read: We speak of A as causing B when the occurrence of B may be inferred from the occurrence of A and the occurrence of B is either subsequent to or simultaneous with the occurrence of A.

But this will not do either. For there are, first of all, cases where from the occurrence of A we may infer the subsequent occurrence of B, yet would not speak of A as causing B. And, secondly, there are cases where from the occurrence of A we may infer the simultaneous occurrence of B, yet would not speak of A as causing B.

Here is an example of the first case. Given (A) that at t_1 a body freely falling *in vacuo* is moving at a speed of 32 feet per second we can infer (B) that at t_2, one second later, it will be moving at 64 feet per second. We might be prepared to say that this inference was in some sense or other a causal inference. But it would be a most unnatural and "strained" use of the word "cause" to say that the body's movement at 64 feet per second at t_2 was caused by its moving at 32 feet per second at t_1. It would be even more unnatural, to take a famous example, to say that the day that will be here in twelve hours' time is caused by the fact that it is now night. Yet, from the present fact, we can certainly infer that in twelve hours' time it will be day.

An example to illustrate the second point. From the fact that a bar of iron is now glowing we can certainly infer (and it will be a causal inference) that it is now at a temperature of 1,000°C. or over. Yet we should not say that its high temperature was caused by the glowing: we say that the high temperature causes the glowing, not *vice-versa*. Another example: watching the voltmeter and battery in the electrical circuit previously described, we see that the needle suddenly jumps, showing that the potential difference has suddenly increased. From this we infer that the electrical resistance of the circuit has, at that moment, increased. But we should not say that the rise in potential difference caused the increase in resistance: rather that the rise in resistance caused a rise in the potential difference. Or, again, knowing the properties of a certain sort of wax, we infer from the fact that the wax has melted that, at that very moment, it reached such and such a temperature. Yet we should not say that the wax's melting caused it to reach the critical temperature: rather that its reaching that temperature caused it to melt.

Why do we speak of "cause" in some cases in which we can infer from A to B, but not in others?

The reason is not always of the same sort. Sometimes in such a case it would be nonsense to speak of A causing B, sometimes it would merely be false. Our very last example is a rather trivial instance of the first sort of reason. It is nonsense to speak of the melting of the wax causing the high temperature of the wax because "x melts" means "high temperature causes x to become liquid." So, "the melting of the wax caused the high-temperature of the wax" is equivalent to the absurdity "the high temperature of the wax's causing of the wax to become liquid caused the high temperature of the wax."

But it is not for this sort of reason that we do not say that the glowing of the iron causes the high temperature of the iron. "Melting" is by definition an effect and not a cause of an increase in temperature, but the same is not true of "glowing." It is not logically absurd to say that the glowing of a piece of iron causes its high temperature; it is merely untrue. It is possible to imagine and to describe a world in which it would have been true. Here is an account of such an imaginary world.

"Our early ancestors many millennia ago discovered that you could make a large range of substances (wood, water, leaves, etc.) glow first blue, then purple, then red by a process of alternately covering them so as to exclude light, then rapidly letting light fall on them, then quickly covering them again, and so on. Wood, for instance, starts glowing after about six minutes of this treatment, and reaches the red stage in about ten minutes. If it is then left in constant daylight or in constant darkness, it gradually fades through purple to blue and then ceases glowing. A number of other substances behave similarly, though the time needed to produce the glowing effect differs somewhat from substance to substance. None of the things that early man thus learnt to make glow, however, suffered any change of temperature in the process. Then, about 1000 B.C., men got hold of samples of fairly pure iron, for the first time. They tried the covering-uncovering technique on it to see if it too, like wood and water, but unlike certain sorts of rock, would glow if manipulated in this way. They found that it would, but that, unlike other substances, iron began to get hot when it started glowing, got hotter still at the purple stage, and when glowing red was very hot indeed. Precise measurements in modern times showed that on reaching the red stage the temperature of iron was 1,000°C. In other respects this imaginary world is just like our world, except that when you put a poker or other non-combustible object in a fire it does not begin to glow, however hot it gets."

Who can doubt that in this imaginary world we should have said that the glowing of the iron caused its temperature to rise, and not *vice-versa?* What, then, are the essential differences between this world and ours, which would lead us to say one thing in one world and another in another?

Human beings can make bodily movements. They do not move their arms, fingers, mouths and so on by doing anything else; they just move them. By making bodily movements men can manipulate things: can lift them, hold them in certain positions, squeeze them, pull them, rub them against each other, and so on. Men discovered that whenever they manipulated certain things in certain ways in certain conditions certain things happened. When you hold a stone in your hand and make certain complex movements of arm and fingers the stone sails through the air approximately in a parabola. When you manipulate two bits of wood and some dry grass for a long time in a certain way the grass catches fire. When you squeeze an egg, it breaks. When you put a stone in the fire it gets hot. Thus, men found out how to produce certain effects by manipulating things in certain ways: how to make an egg break, how to make a stone hot, how to make dry grass catch fire, and so on.

We have a general manipulative technique for making anything hot: we put it on a fire. We find that when we manipulate certain things in this way, such as water in a vessel, it gets hot but does not begin to glow. But we find, too, that certain other things, such as bars of iron, when manipulated in this way do not only get hot, they also, after a while, start to glow. And we have no general manipulative technique for making things glow: the only way to make iron glow is to apply to it the general technique for making things hot. We speak of making iron glow by making it hot, *i.e.*, by applying to it the usual manipulative technique for making things hot, namely, putting on a fire, which in this special case, also makes it glow. We do not speak of making iron hot by making it glow, for we have no general manipulative technique for making things glow. And we say that the high temperature causes the glowing, not *vice-versa*.

In our imaginary world there is a general manipulative technique for making things glow—namely, rapidly alternating exposure to light and shielding from light. There is no other way of making them glow. In general, things manipulated in this way glow, but do not get hot.

Iron, however, glows and gets hot. In this world we speak of making iron hot by making it glow, *i.e.*, by applying to it the usual manipulative technique for making things glow, which, in this special case, also makes it hot. We do not speak of making iron glow by making it hot, for the general manipulative technique of putting things on fires, which makes them hot, does not, in this world, also make things glow. And, in this world, we should say that the glowing causes the high temperature, not *vice-versa*.

What this example shows is the following: When we have a general manipulative technique which results in a certain sort of event, A, we speak of producing A by this technique. (Heating things by putting them on a fire.) When in certain cases application of the general technique for producing A also results in B we speak of producing B by producing A. (Making iron glow by heating it.) And in such a case we speak of A causing B, but not *vice-versa*. Thus, the notion of causation is essentially connected with our manipulative techniques for producing results. Roughly speaking: "A rise in the temperature of iron causes it to glow" means "By applying to iron the general technique for making things hot you will also, in this case, make it glow." And "The glowing of iron causes its temperature to rise" means "By applying to iron the general technique for making things glow you will also, in this case, make it hot." This latter statement is, as it happens, false, for there is no general technique for making things glow, let alone one which, applied to iron, also makes it hot.

Thus, a statement about the cause of something is very closely connected with a recipe for producing it or for preventing it. It is not exactly the same, however. One often makes a remark of the form "A causes B" with the practical aim of telling someone how to produce or prevent B, but not always. Sometimes one wishes to make a theoretical point. And one can sometimes properly say of some particular happening, A, that it caused some other particular event, B, even when no one could have produced A, by manipulation, as a means of producing B. For example, one may say that the rise in mean sea-level at a certain geological epoch was due to the melting of the Polar ice-cap. But when one can properly say this sort of thing it is always the case that people can produce events of the first sort as a means to producing events of the second sort. For example, one can melt ice in order to raise the level of water in a certain area. We could come rather closer to the meaning of "A causes B" if we said: "Events of the B sort can be produced by means of producing events of the A sort."

This account fits in with the principle that an event, A, at time t_2

cannot be the cause of an event, B, at an earlier time, t_1. It is a logical truth that one cannot alter the past. One cannot, therefore, by manipulations at t_2 which produce A at t_2 also produce B retrospectively at t_1.

Let us turn now to the cases where, although from a state of affairs A we can infer a later state of affairs B, we nevertheless would not say that A causes B; *e.g.*, to the case where from the speed of a freely falling body at t_1 we can infer its speed at t_2, or infer coming darkness from present daylight. These are cases where a process is taking place whose law we know, so that we can infer from one stage in the process a later stage. Our inference presupposes that nothing happens to interfere with the process; the falling body will not encounter an obstruction, the earth's spinning will not be stopped by, say, our sun becoming a super-nova. The difference between the earth's spinning and the body's falling is that in the latter case we can set the process going and arrange that nothing shall thereafter interfere with it for a certain time; in the former case we cannot. It is the same sort of difference as there is between melting ice in a bucket and the water-level rising in the bucket and melting Polar ice-caps and sea-level rising. We cannot set the earth spinning, but we can set a top spinning.

Imagine a world in which there is an exact correlation between the colour and the temperature of everything. Anything at a certain low temperature is a certain shade of, say, blue. If an object becomes warmer, its colour changes to purple, then red, then orange, then yellow and finally to white. Cold (or blue) objects can be made hot (or red) by putting them in a fire; after a long time in a very big fire they become very hot (yellow). In such a world we should very probably not have had two sets of words: "cold," "warm," "hot," "very hot" and also "blue," "purple," "red," "yellow"—but only one set—say, the words "blue," "purple," "red," and so on. We should have spoken of things "looking purple," or "being purple to the eyes" and of their "feeling purple" or "being purple to the touch." (In our actual world we talk of things being round or square whether we apprehend their shapes by the eye or by the touch: we do not have a special word meaning "round to the eye" and another quite different word meaning "round to the touch," since there is a correlation between these.)

In such a world we should speak of making purple things red by putting them on a fire, but should not normally speak of making something "red to the eye" (*i.e.*, what we mean by "red") by putting it on a fire; nor of making something "red to the touch" (*i.e.*, what we mean by "hot") by this method. Still less should we speak of making something "red to the eye" by making it "red to the touch," or of making it "red to the touch" by making it "red to the eye." (In our actual world we do not speak of making things "visibly round" by making them "tangibly round," nor *vice-versa*.) When a single manipulation on our part invariably produces two effects A and B, we do not speak of producing one by producing the other, nor do we speak of one as a cause of the other. (The visible roundness is neither cause nor effect of the tangible roundness of a penny.) It is only when we have a technique for producing A which in some circumstances but not in all also produces B that we speak of producing B by producing A, and speak of A as causing B.

When we set a process going—drop a stone from a tower, set a top spinning—we set the stage, see that nothing shall interfere (for a certain time at least) with the process we are about to start, and then set things going. After that, things take their own course without further intervention on our part—the stone gathers speed, the top loses it. There are successive stages in the process. At stage A at t_1 the stone is moving fairly fast, at a later stage B at t_2 the stone is going very fast. But, on the presupposition that the process continues undisturbed, the very same initial stage-setting and send-off C, which will produce fairly fast motion at t_1 (A), will always produce very fast motion at t_2 (B), and the initial stage-setting and send-off C, which will produce very fast motion at t_2 (B), will always produce fairly fast motion at t_1 (A). That is, the process being undisturbed, an initial send-off, C, will always produce both A and B: there is not a general technique for producing A which in some circumstances also produces B. Hence, we do not speak of producing B by producing A. There is not a general technique for bringing it about that, one second after the start, a stone is falling at 32 feet per second, which in some circumstances can also be used to bring it about that two seconds after the start it is falling at 64 feet per second. Hence, we do not speak of achieving the latter by means of the former, and do not speak of the former as causing the latter.

Of course one could, by attaching a rocket to the falling body, which fires one second after the start, secure that a body which is moving at 32 feet per second one second after departure is one second later travelling much faster than 64 feet per second. But this would contradict our presupposition that the process, after being started, was left uninterfered with. It is on this presupposition only that C always produces both A and B.

I have made two points:

First: that one says "A causes B" in cases where one could produce an event or state of the A sort as a means to producing one of the

B sort. I have, that is, explained the "cause-effect" relation in terms of the "producing-by-means-of" relation.

Second: I have tried to give a general account of the producing-by-means-of relation itself: what it is to produce B by producing A. We learn by experience that whenever in certain conditions we manipulate objects in a certain way a certain change, A, occurs. Performing this manipulation is then called: "producing A." We learn also that in certain special cases, or when certain additional conditions are also present, the manipulation in question also results in another sort of change, B. In these cases the manipulation is also called "producing B," and, since it is in general the manipulation of producing A, in this case it is called "producing B by producing A." For example, one makes iron glow by heating it. And I discussed two sorts of case where one does not speak of "producing B by producing A." (1) Where the manipulation for producing A is the general technique for producing B, so that one cannot speak of "producing B by producing A" but only *vice-versa*. (2) Where the given manipulation invariably produces both A and B, so that the manipulation for producing B is not a special case only of that for producing A.

The notion of "cause" here elucidated is the fundamental or primitive one. It is not the property of scientists; except for those whose work most directly bears on such things as engineering, agriculture or medicine, and who are naturally interested in helping their practical colleagues; scientists hardly ever make use of the notion. A statement about causes in the sense here outlined comes very near to being a recipe for producing or preventing certain effects. It is not simply an inference-licence. Professional scientists, when they are carefully stating their findings, mostly express themselves in functional laws, which are pure inference-licences, with nothing of the recipe about them (explicitly at least). Thus the formula $I = \dfrac{E}{R}$ tells you how to infer the current in a given circuit, knowing the electro-motive force and the resistance; it tells you how to infer the electro-motive force, knowing the resistance and current; and how to infer the resistance from current and electro-motive force. All these three things it tells you; and no one of them any more specially than any other—it works all ways, as an inference-licence. But while one might say a current of 3 amps. was caused by an e.m.f. of 6 volts across a resistance of 2 ohms, one would hardly say that a resistance of 2 ohms in the circuit was caused by an e.m.f. of 6 volts and a current of 3 amps. Why not? Given an e.m.f. of 6 volts, one could make 3 amps. flow by making the resistance equal to 2 ohms.

But one could not, given an e.m.f. of 6 volts, make the resistance of the circuit equal to 2 ohms by making a current of 3 amps. flow.

From one point of view the progress of natural science can be viewed as resulting from the substitution of pure inference-licences for recipes.

There is, however, what might be called a "popular science" use of "cause" which may not exactly fit the account given—a use of the word by laymen who know some science and by some scientists in their less strictly professional moments. I have in mind such a locution as "Gravity causes unsupported bodies to fall." Such a statement is not quite on a par, logically, with "Great heat causes steel to melt." It would be fair to say, I think, that the use of the word "cause" here is a sophisticated extension from its more primitive and fundamental meaning. It is the root notion that I have been concerned with.

In accounts of causation given by philosophers in the past a specially fundamental role was often played by the motion of bodies. Every kind of change and every kind of natural law was often supposed to be "ultimately reducible to" or to be explicable in terms of it. In this account, too, though in a rather different way, the motion of bodies occupies a special position. Central to this account is the notion of a manipulation to produce A and thereby to produce B. When we manipulate things we control the motion of bodies; *e.g.*, by rubbing sticks together (motion of bodies) men made them hot and thereby caused them to ignite. At least all those causal chains that are initiated by human beings go back to manipulations, that is, to matter in motion.

HUME'S EXPLANATION
OF INDUCTIVE INFERENCE*

Karl R. Popper

I approached the problem of induction through Hume. Hume, I felt, was perfectly right in pointing out that induction cannot be logically justified. He held that there can be no valid logical[1] arguments allowing us to establish *"that those instances, of which we have had no experience, resemble those, of which we have had experience."* Consequently, *"even after the observation of the frequent or constant conjunction of objects, we have no reason to draw any inference concerning any object beyond those of which we have had experience."* For "shou'd it be said that we have experience"[2]—experience teaching us that objects constantly conjoined with certain other objects continue to be so conjoined—then, Hume says, "I wou'd renew my question, *why from this experience we form any conclusion beyond those past instances, of which we have had experience."* In other words, an attempt to justify the practice of induction by an appeal to experience must lead to an *infinite regress.* As a result, we can say that theories can never be inferred from observation statements, or rationally justified by them.

I found Hume's refutation of inductive inference clear and conclusive. But I felt completely dissatisfied with his psychological explanation of induction in terms of custom or habit.

It has often been noticed that this explanation of Hume's is philosophically not very satisfactory. It is, however, without doubt intended as a *psychological* rather than a philosophical theory; for it tries to give a causal explanation of a psychological fact—*the fact that we believe in*

* From *Conjectures & Refutations* by Karl R. Popper (New York: Basic Books, 1962), pp. 42–46. Reprinted by permission. This is one of several passages discussing Hume in Professor Popper's book.

[1] Hume does not say "logical" but "demonstrative," a terminology which, I think, is a little misleading. The following two quotations are from the *Treatise of Human Nature*, Book I, Part III, sections vi and xii. (The italics are all Hume's.)

[2] This and the next quotation are from *loc. cit.*, section vi. See also Hume's *Enquiry Concerning Human Understanding*, section IV, Part II, and his *Abstract*, edited 1938 by J. M. Keynes and P. Sraffa, p. 15, and quoted in *L.Sc.D.*, new appendix *VII, text to note 6.

laws, in statements asserting regularities or constantly conjoined kinds of events—by asserting that this fact is due to (i.e., constantly conjoined with) custom or habit. But even this reformulation of Hume's theory is still unsatisfactory; for what I have just called a "psychological fact" may itself be described as a custom or habit—the custom or habit of believing in laws or regularities; and it is neither very surprising nor very enlightening to hear that such a custom or habit must be explained as due to, or conjoined with, a custom or habit (even though a different one). Only when we remember that the words "custom" and "habit" are used by Hume, as they are in ordinary language, not merely to *describe* regular behaviour, but rather to *theorize about its origin* (ascribed to frequent repetition), can we reformulate his psychological theory in a more satisfactory way. We can then say that, like other habits, *our habit of believing in laws is the product of frequent repetition*—of the repeated observation that things of a certain kind are constantly conjoined with things of another kind.

This genetico-psychological theory is, as indicated, incorporated in ordinary language, and it is therefore hardly as revolutionary as Hume thought. It is no doubt an extremely popular psychological theory—part of "common sense," one might say. But in spite of my love of both common sense and Hume, I felt convinced that this psychological theory was mistaken; and that it was in fact refutable on purely logical grounds.

Hume's psychology, which is the popular psychology, was mistaken, I felt, about at least three different things: (*a*) the typical result of repetition; (*b*) the genesis of habits; and especially (*c*) the character of those experiences or modes of behaviour which may be described as "believing in a law" or "expecting a law-like succession of events."

(*a*) The typical result of repetition—say, of repeating a difficult passage on the piano—is that movements which at first needed attention are in the end executed without attention. We might say that the process becomes radically abbreviated, and ceases to be conscious: it becomes "physiological." Such a process, far from creating a conscious expectation of law-like succession, or a belief in a law, may on the contrary begin with a conscious belief and destroy it by making it superfluous. In learning to ride a bicycle, we may start with the belief that we can avoid falling if we steer in the direction in which we threaten to fall, and this belief may be useful for guiding our movements. After sufficient practice we may forget the rule; in any case, we do not need it any longer. On the other hand, even if it is true that repetition may create unconscious expectations, these become conscious only if something goes wrong (we may not have heard the clock tick, but we may hear that it has stopped).

(*b*) Habits or customs do not, as a rule, *originate* in repetition. Even the habit of walking, or of speaking, or of feeding at certain hours, *begins* before repetition can play any part whatever. We may say, if we like, that they deserve to be called "habits" or "customs" only after repetition has played its typical part; but we must not say that the practices in question originated as the result of many repetitions.

(*c*) Belief in a law is not quite the same thing as behaviour which betrays an expectation of a law-like succession of events; but these two are sufficiently closely connected to be treated together. They may, perhaps, in exceptional cases, result from a mere repetition of sense impressions (as in the case of the stopping clock). I was prepared to concede this, but I contended that normally, and in most cases of any interest, they cannot be so explained. As Hume admits, even a single striking observation may be sufficient to create a belief or an expectation—a fact which he tries to explain as due to an inductive habit, formed as the result of a vast number of long repetitive sequences which had been experienced at an earlier period of life.[3] But this, I contended, was merely his attempt to explain away unfavourable facts which threatened his theory; an unsuccessful attempt, since these unfavourable facts could be observed in very young animals and babies—as early, indeed, as we like. "A lighted cigarette was held near the noses of the young puppies," reports F. Bäge. "They sniffed at it once, turned tail, and nothing would induce them to come back to the source of the smell and to sniff again. A few days later, they reacted to the mere sight of a cigarette or even of a rolled piece of white paper, by bounding away, and sneezing."[4] If we try to explain cases like this by postulating a vast number of long repetitive sequences at a still earlier age, we are not only romancing, but forgetting that in the clever puppies' short lives there must be room not only for repetition but also for a great deal of novelty, and consequently of non-repetition.

But it is not only that certain empirical facts do not support Hume; there are decisive arguments of a *purely logical* nature against his psychological theory.

The central idea of Hume's theory is that of *repetition, based upon similarity* (or "resemblance"). This idea is used in a very uncritical way.

---

[3] *Treatise*, section xiii; section xv, rule 4.
[4] F. Bäge, "Zur Entwicklung, etc.," *Zeitschrift f. Hundeforschung*, 1933; cp. D. Katz, *Animals and Men*, ch. vi, footnote.

We are led to think of the water-drop that hollows the stone: of se-quences of unquestionably like events slowly forcing themselves upon us, as does the tick of the clock. But we ought to realize that in a psychological theory such as Hume's, only repetition-for-us, based upon similarity-for-us, can be allowed to have any effect upon us. We must respond to situations as if they were equivalent; *take* them as similar; *interpret* them as repetitions. The clever puppies, we may as-sume, showed by their response, their way of acting or of reacting, that they recognized or interpreted the second situation as a repetition of the first: that they expected its main element, the objectionable smell, to be present. The situation was a repetition-for-them because they re-sponded to it by *anticipating* its similarity to the previous one.

This apparently psychological criticism has a purely logical basis which may be summed up in the following simple argument. (It hap-pens to be the one from which I originally started my criticism.) The kind of repetition envisaged by Hume can never be perfect; the cases he has in mind cannot be cases of perfect sameness; they can only be cases of similarity. Thus *they are repetitions only from a certain point of view.* (What has the effect upon me of a repetition may not have this effect upon a spider.) But this means that, for logical reasons, there must always be a point of view—such as a system of expectations, antici-pations, assumptions, or interests—*before* there can be any repetition; which point of view, consequently, cannot be merely the result of repetition.

We must thus replace, for the purposes of a psychological theory of the origin of our beliefs, the naïve idea of events which *are* similar by the idea of events to which we react by *interpreting* them as being similar. But if this is so (and I can see no escape from it), then Hume's psychological theory of induction leads to an infinite regress, precisely analogous to that other infinite regress which was discovered by Hume himself, and used by him to explode the logical theory of induction. For, what do we wish to explain? In the example of the puppies we wish to explain behaviour which may be described as *recognizing or interpret-ing* a situation as a repetition of another. Clearly, we cannot hope to explain this by an appeal to earlier repetitions, once we realize that the earlier repetitions must also have been repetitions-for-them, so that precisely the same problem arises again: that of *recognizing or inter-preting* a situation as a repetition of another.

To put it more concisely, similarity-for-us is the product of a response involving interpretations (which may be inadequate) and anticipations or expectations (which may never be fulfilled). It is there-for impossible to explain anticipations, or expectations, as resulting from many repetitions, as suggested by Hume. For even the first repetition-for-us must be based upon similarity-for-us, and therefore upon expectations—precisely the kind of thing we wished to explain.

This shows that there is an infinite regress involved in Hume's psychological theory.

Hume, I felt, had never accepted the full force of his own logical analysis. Having refuted the logical idea of induction, he was faced with the following problem: how do we actually obtain our knowledge, as a matter of psychological fact, if induction is a procedure which is logically invalid and rationally unjustifiable? There are two possible answers: (1) We obtain our knowledge by a non-inductive procedure. This answer would have allowed Hume to retain a form of rationalism. (2) We obtain our knowledge by repetition and induction, and therefore by a logically invalid and rationally unjustifiable procedure, so that all apparent knowledge is merely a kind of belief—belief based on habit. This answer would imply that even scientific knowledge is irrational, so that rationalism is absurd, and must be given up. (I shall not discuss here the age-old attempts, now again fashionable, to get out of the difficulty by asserting that though induction is of course logically invalid if we mean by "logic" the same as "deductive logic," it is not irrational by its own standards, as may be seen from the fact that every reasonable man applies it *as a matter of fact*: it was Hume's great achievement to break this uncritical identification of the question of fact—*quid facti*—and the question of justification or validity—*quid juris*.)

It seems that Hume never seriously considered the first alternative. Having cast out the logical theory of induction by repetition, he struck a bargain with common sense, meekly allowing the re-entry of induction by repetition, in the guise of a psychological theory. I proposed to turn the tables upon this theory of Hume's. Instead of explaining our propensity to expect regularities as the result of repetition, I proposed to explain repetition-for-us as the result of our propensity to expect regularities and to search for them.

Thus, I was led by purely logical considerations to replace the psychological theory of induction by the following view. Without waiting, passively, for repetitions to impress or impose regularities upon us, we actively try to impose regularities upon the world. We try to discover similarities in it, and to interpret it in terms of laws invented by us. Without waiting for premises we jump to conclusions. These may have to be discarded later, should observation show that they are wrong.

This was a theory of trial and error—of *conjectures and refutations*. It made it possible to understand why our attempts to force interpretations upon the world were logically prior to the observation of similarities. Since there were logical reasons behind this procedure, I thought that it would apply in the field of science also; that scientific theories were not the digest of observations, but that they were inventions—conjectures boldly put forward for trial, to be eliminated if they clashed with observations; with observations which were rarely accidental but as a rule undertaken with the definite intention of testing a theory by obtaining, if possible, a decisive refutation.

THE JUSTIFICATION OF
INDUCTION*

P. F. Strawson

If someone asked what grounds there were for supposing that deductive reasoning was valid, we might answer that there were in fact no grounds for supposing that deductive reasoning was always valid; sometimes people made valid inferences, and sometimes they were guilty of logical fallacies. If he said that we had misunderstood his question, and that what he wanted to know was what grounds there were for regarding deduction *in general* as a valid method of argument, we should have to answer that his question was without sense, for to say that an argument, or a form or method of argument, was valid or invalid would *imply* that it was deductive; the concepts of validity and invalidity had application only to individual deductive arguments or forms of deductive argument. Similarly, if a man asked what grounds there were for thinking it reasonable to hold beliefs arrived at inductively, one might at first answer that there were good and bad inductive arguments, that sometimes it was reasonable to hold a belief arrived at inductively and sometimes it was not. If he, too, said that his question had been misunderstood, that he wanted to know whether induction in general was a reasonable method of inference, then we might well think his question senseless in the same way as the question whether deduction is in general valid; for to call a particular belief reasonable or unreasonable is to apply inductive standards, just as to call a particular argument valid or invalid is to apply deductive standards. The parallel is not wholly convincing; for words like "reasonable" and "rational" have not so precise and technical a sense as the word "valid." Yet it is sufficiently powerful to make us wonder how the second question could be raised at all, to wonder why, in contrast with the corresponding question about deduction, it should have seemed to constitute a genuine problem.

* From *Introduction to Logical Theory* by P. F. Strawson (New York: John Wiley & Sons, Inc., 1952), pp. 249–263. Reprinted by permission of John Wiley & Sons, Inc.

Suppose that a man is brought up to regard formal logic as the study of the science and art of reasoning. He observes that all inductive processes are, by deductive standards, invalid; the premises never entail the conclusions. Now, inductive processes are notoriously important in the formation of beliefs and expectations about everything which lies beyond the observation of available witnesses. But an *invalid* argument is an *unsound* argument; an *unsound* argument is one in which *no good reason* is produced for accepting the conclusion. So, if inductive processes are invalid, if all the arguments we should produce, if challenged, in support of our beliefs about what lies beyond the observation of available witnesses are unsound, then we have no good reason for any of these beliefs. This conclusion is repugnant. So there arises the demand for a justification, not of this or that particular belief which goes beyond what is entailed by our evidence, but a justification of induction in general. And when the demand arises in this way it is, in effect, the demand that induction shall be shown to be really a kind of deduction; for nothing less will satisfy the doubter when this is the route to his doubts.

Tracing this, the most common route to the general doubt about the reasonableness of induction, shows how the doubt seems to escape the absurdity of a demand that induction in general shall be justified by inductive standards. The demand is that induction should be shown to be a rational process; and this turns out to be the demand that one kind of reasoning should be shown to be another and different kind. Put thus crudely, the demand seems to escape one absurdity only to fall into another. Of course, inductive arguments are not deductively valid; if they were, they would be deductive arguments. Inductive reasoning must be assessed, for soundness, by inductive standards. Nevertheless, fantastic as the wish for induction to be deduction may seem, it is only in terms of it that we can understand some of the attempts that have been made to justify induction. . . .

I shall . . . consider a . . . sophisticated kind of attempt to justify induction . . . The aim envisaged is that of proving that the probability of a generalization, whether universal or proportional, increases with the number of instances for which it is found to hold. . . . Suppose we had a collection of objects of different kinds, some with some characteristics and some with others. Suppose, for example, we had a bag containing 100 balls, of which 70 were white and 30 black. Let us call such a collection of objects a *population;* and let us call the way it is made up (e.g., in the case imagined, of 70 white and 30 black balls) the *constitution* of the population. From such a population it would be possible to take *samples* of various sizes. For example, we might take from our bag a sample of 30 balls. Suppose each ball in the bag had an individual number. Then the collection of balls numbered 10 to 39 inclusive would be one sample of the given size; the collection of balls numbered 11 to 40 inclusive would be another and different sample of the same size; the collection of balls numbered 2, 4, 6, 8 . . . 58, 60 would be another such sample; and so on. Each possible collection of 30 balls is a different sample of the same size. Some different samples of the same size will have the same constitutions as one another; others will have different constitutions. Thus there will be only one sample made up of 30 black balls. There will be many different samples which share the constitution: 20 white and 10 black. It would be a simple matter of mathematics to work out the number of possible samples of the given size which had any one possible constitution. Let us say that a sample *matches* the population if, allowing for the difference between them in size, the constitution of the sample corresponds, within certain limits, to that of the population. For example, we might say that any possible sample consisting of, say, 21 white and 9 black balls matched the constitution (70 white and 30 black) of the population, whereas a sample consisting of 20 white and 10 black balls did not. Now it is a proposition of pure mathematics that, given any population, the proportion of possible samples, all of the same size, which match the population, increases with the size of the sample.

Conclusions about the ratio of a subset of equally possible chances to the whole set of those chances may be expressed by the use of the word "probability." Thus, of the 52 possible samples of one card from a population constituted like an orthodox pack, 16 are court-cards or aces. This fact we allow ourselves to express (under the conditions, inductively established, of equipossibility of draws) by saying that the probability of drawing a court-card or an ace was $4/13$. If we express the proposition referred to at the end of the last paragraph by means of this use of "probability," we shall obtain the result: The probability of a sample matching a given population increases with the size of the sample. It is tempting to try to derive from this result a general justification of the inductive procedure: which will not, indeed, show that any given inductive conclusion is entailed by the evidence for it, taken in conjunction with some universal premise, but will show that the multiplication of favourable instances of a generalization entails a proportionate increase in its probability. For, since *matching* is a symmetrical relation, it might seem a simple deductive step to move from

    I. The probability of a sample matching a given population increases with the size of the sample

to

    II. The probability of a population matching a given sample increases with the size of the sample.

II might seem to provide a guarantee that the greater the number of cases for which a generalization is observed to hold, the greater is its probability; since in increasing the number of cases we increase the size of the sample from whatever population forms the subject of our generalization. Thus, pure mathematics might seem to provide the sought-for proof that the evidence for a generalization really does get stronger, the more favourable instances of it we find.

    The argument is ingenious enough to be worthy of respect; but it fails of its purpose, and misrepresents the inductive situation. Our situation is not in the least like that of a man drawing a sample from a given, i.e., fixed and limited, population from which the drawing of any mathematically possible sample is equiprobable with that of any other. Our only datum is the sample. No limit is fixed beforehand to the diversity, and the possibilities of change, of the "population" from which it is drawn: or, better, to the multiplicity and variousness of different populations, each with different constitutions, any one of which might replace the present one before we make the next draw. Nor is there any *a priori* guarantee that different mathematically possible samples are equally likely to be drawn. If we have or can obtain any assurance on these points, then it is assurance derived inductively from our data, and cannot therefore be assumed at the outset of an argument designed to justify induction. So II, regarded as a justification of induction founded on purely mathematical considerations, is a fraud. The important shift of "given" from qualifying "population" in I to qualifying "sample" in II is illegitimate. Moreover, "probability," which means one thing in II (interpreted as giving the required guarantee), means something quite different in I (interpreted as a proposition of pure mathematics). In I probability is simply the measure of the ratio of one set of mathematically possible chances to another; in II it is the measure of the inductive acceptability of a generalization. As a mathematical proposition, I is certainly independent of the soundness of inductive procedures; and as a statement of one of the criteria we use in assessing the strength of evidence of a generalization, II is as certainly independent of mathematics.

It has not escaped the notice of those who have advocated a mathematical justification of induction that certain assumptions are required to make the argument even seem to fulfill its purpose. Inductive reasoning would be of little use if it did not sometimes enable us to assign at least fairly high probabilities to certain conclusions. Now suppose, in conformity with the mathematical model, we represented the fact that the evidence for a proposition was conclusive by assigning to it the probability figure of 1; and the fact that the evidence for and against a proposition was evenly balanced by assigning to it the probability figure $\frac{1}{2}$; and so on. It is a familiar mathematical truth that, between any two fractions, say $\frac{1}{6}$ and $\frac{1}{5}$, there is an infinite number of intermediate quantities; that $\frac{1}{6}$ can be indefinitely increased without reaching equality to $\frac{1}{5}$. Even if we could regard II as mathematically established, therefore, it fails to give us what we require; for it fails to provide a guarantee that the probability of an inductive conclusion ever attains a degree at which it begins to be of use. . . .

Let us turn from attempts to justify induction to attempts to show that the demand for a justification is mistaken. We have seen already that what lies behind such a demand is often the absurd wish that induction should be shown to be some kind of deduction—and this wish is clearly traceable in the two attempts at justification which we have examined. What other sense could we give to the demand? Sometimes it is expressed in the form of a request for proof that induction is a *reasonable* or *rational* procedure, that we have *good grounds* for placing reliance upon it. Consider the uses of the phrases "good grounds," "justification," "reasonable," &c. Often we say such things as "He has *every justification* for believing that *p*"; "I have *very good reasons* for believing it"; "There are *good grounds* for the view that *q*"; "There is *good evidence* that *r*." We often talk, in such ways as these, of justification, good grounds or reasons or evidence for certain beliefs. Suppose such a belief were one expressible in the form "Every case of *f* is a case of *g*." And suppose someone were asked what he meant by saying that he had good grounds or reasons for holding it. I think it would be felt to be a satisfactory answer if he replied: "Well, in all my wide and varied experience I've come across innumerable cases of *f* and never a case of *f* which wasn't a case of *g*." In saying this, he is clearly claiming to have *inductive* support, *inductive* evidence, of a certain kind, for his belief; and he is also giving a perfectly proper answer to the question, what he meant by saying that he had ample justification, good grounds, good reasons for his belief. It is an analytic proposition that it is reasonable to have a degree of belief in a statement which is proportional to the strength of the evidence in its favour; and it is an analytic proposition, though not a proposition of mathematics, that, other things being equal, the evidence for a generalization is strong in proportion as the number of favourable instances, and the variety of circumstances in which they have been found, are great. So, to ask whether it is reasonable to place reliance on inductive procedures is like asking whether it is reasonable to proportion the degree of one's convictions to the strength of the evidence. Doing this is what "being reasonable" *means* in such a context.

As for the other form in which the doubt may be expressed, viz., "Is induction a justified, or justifiable, procedure?" it emerges in a still less favourable light. No sense has been given to it, though it is easy to see why it seems to have a sense. For it is generally proper to inquire *of a particular belief* whether its adoption is justified; and, in asking this, we are asking whether there is good, bad, or any, evidence for it. In applying or withholding the epithets "justified," "well founded," &c., in the case of specific beliefs, we are appealing to, and applying, inductive standards. But to what standards are we appealing when we ask whether the application of inductive standards is justified or well grounded? If we cannot answer, then no sense has been given to the question. Compare it with the question: Is the law legal? It makes perfectly good sense to inquire of a particular action, of an administrative regulation, or even, in the case of some states, of a particular enactment of the legislature, whether or not it is legal. The question is answered by an appeal to a legal system, by the application of a set of legal (or constitutional) rules or standards. But it makes no sense to inquire in general whether the law of the land, the legal system as a whole, is or is not legal. For to what legal standards are we appealing?

The only way in which a sense might be given to the question, whether induction is in general a justified or justifiable procedure, is a trivial one which we have already noticed. We might interpret it to mean "Are all conclusions, arrived at inductively, justified?" i.e., "Do people always have adequate evidence for the conclusions they draw?" The answer to this question is easy, but uninteresting: it is that sometimes people have adequate evidence, and sometimes they do not.

It seems, however, that this way of showing the request for a general justification of induction to be absurd is sometimes insufficient to allay the worry that produces it. And to point out that "forming rational opinions about the unobserved on the evidence available" and "assessing the evidence by inductive standards" are phrases which describe the same thing, is more apt to produce irritation than relief. The point is felt to be "merely a verbal" one; and though the point of this protest is itself hard to see, it is clear that something more is required. So the question must be pursued further. First, I want to point out that there is something a little odd about talking of "the inductive method," or even "the inductive policy," as if it were just one possible method among others of arguing from the observed to the unobserved, from the available evidence to the facts in question. If one asked a meteorologist what method or methods he used to forecast the weather, one would be surprised if he answered: "Oh, just the inductive method." If one asked a doctor by what means he diagnosed a certain disease, the answer "By induction" would be felt as an impatient evasion, a joke, or a rebuke. The answer one hopes for is an account of the tests made, the signs taken account of, the rules and recipes and general laws applied. When such a specific method of prediction or diagnosis is in question, one can ask whether the method is justified in practice; and here again one is asking whether its employment is inductively justified, whether it commonly gives correct results. This question would normally seem an admissible one. One might be tempted to conclude that, while there are many different specific methods of prediction, diagnosis, &c., appropriate to different subjects of inquiry, all such methods could properly be called "inductive" in the sense that their employment rested on inductive support; and that, hence, the phrase "non-inductive method of finding out about what lies deductively beyond the evidence" was a description without meaning, a phrase to which no sense had been given; so that there could be no question of justifying our selection of one method, called "the inductive," of doing this.

However, someone might object: "Surely it is possible, though it might be foolish, to use methods utterly different from accredited scientific ones. Suppose a man, whenever he wanted to form an opinion about what lay beyond his observation or the observation of available witnesses, simply shut his eyes, asked himself the appropriate question, and accepted the first answer that came into his head. Wouldn't this be a non-inductive method?" Well, let us suppose this. The man is asked: "Do you usually get the right answer by your method?" He might answer: "You've mentioned one of its drawbacks; I never do get the right answer; but it's an extremely easy method." One might then be inclined to think that it was not a method of finding things out at all. But suppose he answered: Yes, it's usually (always) the right answer. Then we might be willing to call it a method of finding out, though a strange one. But, then, by the very fact of its success, it would be an inductively supported method. For each application of the method would be an application of the general rule, "The first answer that comes into my head is generally (always) the right one"; and for the truth of this generalization there would be the inductive evidence of a long run of favourable instances with no unfavourable ones (if it were "always"), or of a sustained high proportion of successes to trials (if it were "generally").

So every successful method or recipe for finding out about the unobserved must be one which has inductive support; for to say that a recipe is successful is to say that it has been repeatedly applied with success; and repeated successful application of a recipe constitutes just what we mean by inductive evidence in its favour. Pointing out this fact must not be confused with saying that "the inductive method" is justified by its success, justified because it works. This is a mistake, and an important one. I am not seeking to "justify the inductive method," for no meaning has been given to this phrase. *A fortiori,* I am not saying that induction is justified by its success in finding out about the unobserved. I am saying, rather, that any successful method of finding out about the unobserved is necessarily justified by induction. This is an analytic proposition. The phrase "successful method of finding things out which has no inductive support" is self-contradictory. Having, or acquiring, inductive support is a necessary condition of the success of a method.

Why point this out at all? First, it may have a certain therapeutic force, a power to reassure. Second, it may counteract the tendency to think of "the inductive method" as something on a par with specific methods of diagnosis or prediction and therefore, like them, standing in need of (inductive) justification.

There is one further confusion, perhaps the most powerful of all in producing the doubts, questions, and spurious solutions discussed in this Part. We may approach it by considering the claim that induction is justified by its success in practice. The phrase "success of induction" is by no means clear and perhaps embodies the confusion of induction with some specific method of prediction, &c., appropriate to some particular line of inquiry. But, whatever the phrase may mean, the claim has an obviously circular look. Presumably the suggestion is that we should argue from the past "successes of induction" to the continuance of those successes in the future; from the fact that it has worked hitherto to the conclusion that it will continue to work. Since an argument of this kind is plainly inductive, it will not serve as a justification of induction. One cannot establish a principle of argument by an argument which uses that principle. But let us go a little deeper. The argument rests the justification of induction on a matter of fact (its "past successes"). This is characteristic of nearly all attempts to find a justification. . . . Even the mathematical argument [earlier] required buttressing with some large assumption about the make-up of the world. I think the source of this general desire to find out some fact about the constitution of the universe which will "justify induction" or "show it to be a rational policy" is the confusion, the running together, of two fundamentally different questions: to one of which the answer is a matter of non-linguistic fact, while to the other it is a matter of meanings.

There is nothing self-contradictory in supposing that all the uniformities in the course of things that we have hitherto observed and come to count on should cease to operate to-morrow; that all our familiar recipes should let us down, and that we should be unable to frame new ones because such regularities as there were were too complex for us to make out. (We may assume that even the expectation that all of us, in such circumstances, would perish were falsified by someone surviving to observe the new chaos in which, roughly speaking, nothing foreseeable happens.) Of course, we do not believe that this will happen. We believe, on the contrary, that our inductively supported expectation-rules, though some of them will have, no doubt, to be dropped or modified, will continue, on the whole, to serve us fairly well; and that we shall generally be able to replace the rules we abandon with others similarly arrived at. We might give a sense to the phrase "success of induction" by calling this vague belief the belief that induction will continue to be successful. It is certainly a factual belief, not a necessary truth; a belief, one may say, about the constitution of the universe. We might express it as follows, choosing a phraseology which will serve the better to expose the confusion I wish to expose:

I. (The universe is such that) induction will continue to be successful.

I is very vague: it amounts to saying that there are, and will continue to be, natural uniformities and regularities which exhibit a humanly manageable degree of simplicity. But, though it is vague, certain definite things can be said about it. (1) It is not a necessary, but a contingent, statement; for chaos is not a self-contradictory concept. (2) We have good inductive reasons for believing it, good inductive evidence for it. We believe that some of our recipes will continue to hold good because they have held good for so long. We believe that we shall be able to

frame new and useful ones, because we have been able to do so repeatedly in the past. Of course, it would be absurd to try to use I to
"justify induction," to show that it is a reasonable policy; because I is a
conclusion inductively supported.

Consider now the fundamentally different statement:

II. Induction is rational (reasonable).

We have already seen that the rationality of induction, unlike its "suc-
cessfulness," is not a fact about the constitution of the world. It is a
matter of what we mean by the word "rational" in its application to any
procedure for forming opinions about what lies outside our observations or that of available witnesses. For to have good reasons for any
such opinion is to have good inductive support for it. The chaotic universe just envisaged, therefore, is not one in which induction would
cease to be rational; it is simply one in which it would be impossible to
form rational expectations to the effect that specific things would happen. It might be said that in such a universe it would at least be rational
to refrain from forming specific expectations, to expect nothing but
irregularities. Just so. But this is itself a higher-order induction: where
irregularity is the rule, expect further irregularities. Learning not to
count on things is as much learning an inductive lesson as learning what
things to count on.

So it is a contingent, factual matter that it is sometimes possible to
form rational opinions concerning what specifically happened or will
happen in given circumstances (I); it is a non-contingent, *a priori*
matter that the only ways of doing this must be inductive ways (II).
What people have done is to run together, to conflate, the question to
which I is an answer and the quite different question to which II is an
answer; producing the muddled and senseless questions: "Is the universe
such that inductive procedures are rational?" or "What must the universe be like in order for inductive procedures to be rational?" It is the
attempt to answer these confused questions which leads to statements
like "The uniformity of nature is a presupposition of the validity of
induction." The statement that nature is uniform might be taken to be
a vague way of expressing what we expressed by I; and certainly this
fact is a condition of, for it is identical with, the likewise contingent
fact that we are, and shall continue to be, able to form rational opinions,
of the kind we are most anxious to form, about the unobserved. But
neither this fact about the world, nor any other, is a condition of the
necessary truth that, if it is possible to form rational opinions of this
kind, these will be inductively supported opinions. The discordance of

the conflated questions manifests itself in an uncertainty about the status to be accorded to the alleged presupposition of the "validity" of induction. For it was dimly, and correctly, felt that the reasonableness of inductive procedures was not merely a contingent, but a necessary matter; so any necessary condition of their reasonableness had likewise to be a necessary matter. On the other hand, it was uncomfortably clear that chaos is not a self-contradictory concept; that the fact that some phenomena do exhibit a tolerable degree of simplicity and repetitiveness is not guaranteed by logic, but is a contingent affair. So the presupposition of induction had to be both contingent and necessary: which is absurd. And the absurdity is only lightly veiled by the use of the phrase "synthetic *a priori*" instead of "contingent necessary."

HUME'S THEORY OF THE CREDIBILITY OF MIRACLES*

C. D. Broad

☼

§1. Hume's *Essay on Miracles* is, perhaps, the most notorious of his works to the non-philosophic but educated public. Yet its notoriety is mainly due to what has been said about it, and to what it is believed to contain. Probably few people read it who are not making a special study of Hume's philosophy. It has always seemed to me to be an over-rated work, and to fall below the extremely high standard of Hume's other philosophical writings. In the present paper I propose to do three things: (*a*) to state Hume's theory as clearly and fairly as possible; (*b*) to discuss its internal consistency and truth; and (*c*) to see how far it is compatible with Hume's own views about causation and belief.

§2. Hume's argument about the credibility of miraculous stories is closely connected with his theory of causation. It may be put as follows. We believe a great many things on testimony, *i.e.*, because other people tell us that they witnessed the events in question. Why do we believe on testimony? It is because a long experience has taught us that, as a rule, people with no special motive for lying, and with no special cause for self-deception, report accurately in the main what they have observed. We ourselves have verified this conjunction between reports and things reported in a number of cases, *e.g.*, a man tells us that he has seen something (X) at the other side of the town. We go and look, and see it for ourselves. Here we have a conjunction between a fact (X) and the man's testimony to the fact. We find such conjunctions to hold in a great many cases, and it is because we have found this to be so that we generally attach credit to a story if there be no reason for thinking that our informant is specially given to lying or specially liable to make mistakes.

The point that Hume wants us to notice is that our belief in testimony is of exactly the same kind as our belief in causal laws. I believe

---

* From *Proceedings of the Aristotelian Society*, New Series, XVII (1916–1917), 77–94. Reprinted by permission.

that A will always be followed by B because I have so often observed A to be followed by B. I believe what a sensible and truthful man tells me as having been witnessed by himself, because in so many cases where I have been able to make the test I have been able to observe what such men have reported to me. We may compare the observed agreements between such men's accounts and the facts in the past with the observed sequences A and B. And we may compare my general belief that their stories are to be accepted with my belief that A will always be followed by B.

§3. Now, Hume says, it is a general principle that we ought to increase our belief in anything proportionally to the amount of evidence for it and to decrease our belief proportionally to the amount of evidence against it. If in 99 cases out of 100 A has been observed to be followed by B, and in one case B was observed not to follow, we very strongly expect A to be followed by B in the next case. But if this sequence has only happened in 50 per cent of the observed cases, we ought to have no strong expectation of its happening in the next instance. Let us, then, apply this principle to the credibility of stories believed on the evidence of witnesses.

§4. In the first place, the witnesses may conflict with each other. Then we naturally cannot attach much weight to what either party says, because we have just as much cause to believe that the event did not take place as that it did.

But suppose the witnesses all agree in saying that a certain event took place. Then our belief will depend on two factors: (*a*) It will be strengthened by the agreement of the witnesses because we know that, in the majority of cases, when honest and independent witnesses agree in saying that something has happened, that event has happened; (*b*) It will be strengthened or weakened according as the event reported is one that is in itself likely or unlikely to have happened. If I know that events of the kind which the witnesses report have often happened, I have no reason to doubt what they say. But, if they report something that is quite contrary to what has generally been observed to happen, I ought not to believe at all strongly that they are right. For I shall entertain conflicting states of mind. (*a*) I know that what they report is at variance with what generally happens. Hence, I have so far a tendency to believe the contrary of what they report. (*b*) I know that what is reported by a number of honest witnesses is oftener true than false. Hence, I have so far a tendency to believe what they report. These two tendencies, both founded on the same general principle and therefore equally justifiable, will have to fight in my mind; and my final state of belief will be a compromise between the two. It will be weaker than if I attended solely to the agreement of the witnesses, and it will be stronger than if I attended solely to the rarity of the event which they report.

§5. Let us now suppose that the event which is reported is not merely extraordinary but miraculous. What ought we to believe? Hume defines a miracle as follows: It is a transgression of a law of nature by a particular volition of the Deity or by the interposition of some invisible agent. *E.g.*, it would be extraordinary if we were to find a lion in the Great Court at Trinity, or an intelligent and honest man in the Anti-German Union. But such events would not be miracles, because it would be possible to explain even the latter in terms of known laws of nature. It would, however, be a miracle if a lion were to come into my rooms through the keyhole, or a member of the Anti-German Union were to turn Mr. Arthur Ponsonby into a pillar of salt by merely looking at him, for such events are contrary to known laws of nature. Now a law of nature is simply a regularity which has, up to the present, never been known to fail. So Hume says: Any event that is called a miracle either is of a kind that has been observed in other cases or not. If it has been observed in other cases, it is not really a miracle, for it cannot contradict a genuine law of nature. If it never has been observed in other cases, it is a genuine miracle, but there is an absolutely uniform experience against it. So, if any event could justly be called a miracle and not merely an extraordinary occurrence, it must be one which is contrary to the entire course of experience.

Now suppose that a number of honest people agree in asserting that they witnessed a miracle, an event contrary to the whole course of experience. Then, if we consider the reported event by itself, we have the strongest ground for disbelieving in it that we can possibly have. For we have the strongest possible ground for believing in what is incompatible with it, *viz.*, the ground of an absolutely uniform experience. Let us consider the evidence for it. We cannot say that we have the strongest possible ground for believing what honest witnesses agree in telling us, for we know that there are plenty of cases where such witnesses have been mistaken.

So Hume's argument comes to this. Against belief in any alleged miracle we have, by definition of the word miracle, an absolutely uniform experience. For believing in the miracle we have only our experience as to the trustworthiness of testimony. And this is not an absolutely uniform experience, however trustworthy we may suppose the witnesses to be. Therefore, we have never the right to believe in any alleged miracle however strong the testimony for it may be.

§6. Hume says that he has here put the case for miracles as strongly as he can, and has shown that, *however good* the testimony may be, we ought not to believe them. He now goes on to show that the testimony for a miracle never really is the best possible. (1) The witnesses to any alleged miracle have never been at once so well educated as to ensure that they shall not be deluding themselves and so unquestionably honest as to ensure that they are not trying to delude other people. And no alleged miracle has been performed so publicly as to make it certain that no fraud has been employed. (2) Many people have strong motives for believing in miracles. Most people have a fondness for what is wonderful and out of the common, and therefore have a natural tendency to believe any miraculous story on very slight evidence. And a religious enthusiast demands very much less proof for the alleged miracles of his own religion than for those of any other religion or for quite ordinary stories about everyday affairs. (I myself have a Scottish friend who believes all the miracles of the New Testament, but cannot be induced to believe, on the repeated evidence of my own eyes, that a small section of the main North British Railway between Dundee and Aberdeen consists of a single line.) (3) It is rather ominous for miracles that they are almost ostentatiously frequent in barbarous times and among backward peoples, but become fewer and fewer as people become more educated. This strongly suggests that the alleged miracles are due to the ease with which barbaric people are duped by others, and to their lack of knowledge of natural laws, which makes them think that many perfectly natural events (*e.g.*, the firing of a gun) are miraculous.

(4) Lastly, Hume has a very ingenious argument about religious miracles. Any two religious systems, *e.g.*, Christianity and Mahometanism, are incompatible with each other. Any evidence for a Mahometan miracle tends to support Mahometanism, and therefore tends so far to refute Christianity and thus to discredit the evidence for Christian miracles. Similarly, any evidence for a Christian miracle tends to discredit the evidence for Mahometan miracles. Thus, the fact that miracles are alleged to occur in a number of incompatible religions tends to decrease the probability that miracles happen anywhere.

This argument is somewhat subtle, and it contains a suppressed premise; so it will be well to state it more formally. Let R_1 and R_2 be two incompatible religions. And let it be supposed that miracles *only* occur in connexion with *true* religion. (This is the suppressed premise.)

Then the assertion "Miracles occur in connexion with R_1," implies that R_1 is true; this implies that R_2 is false; and this implies that miracles do not occur in connexion with R_2. Similarly, the assertion "Miracles occur in connexion with R_2," implies that miracles do not occur in connexion with R_1. Now both these assertions are made (though, of course, by different sets of people). The combined proposition implies its own contradictory and therefore *must* be false, and therefore *one* of the separate assertions *must* be false, and *both* may be. This argument, however, as we have seen, needs the premise that miracles only occur in connexion with true religion. Now this might very well be false, and it is certainly not universally held by people who believe in religious miracles. Thus, the early Christians accepted the miracles of Pagan religions, but ascribed them to devils.

Hume's final conclusion, then, is that no human testimony, however strong, ought to make us believe a miracle, and that the actual testimony that we are offered for alleged historical miracles is not even the strongest kind of human testimony.

§7. I pass to a consideration of these views. Two distinct questions arise: (*a*) Is Hume right in his arguments and conclusions? (*b*) Are they consistent with his other views, particularly his theories as to belief and causation?

All Hume's arguments to show that the testimony that is actually offered for any particular alleged miracle is untrustworthy seem to me to be sound and important. Investigations made since Hume's time have only strengthened his arguments. We are perhaps less inclined to lay stress on conscious deception carried out "by Priests and Kings for the enslavement of Peoples" than were our forefathers in the eighteenth century. But the careful investigations of the Society for Psychical Research on the extraordinary discrepancies between what intelligent people, who knew that they were looking at mere conjuring tricks, saw, and what they thought they saw, have shown that we must allow far more for honest self-deception than could possibly have been imagined in Hume's time. And perhaps we may mention the celebrated story of the 80,000 Russians who passed through England at the beginning of the war in the presence of such a cloud of witnesses as a case which renders it practically impossible in future to accept a miraculous story *merely* on the evidence of *direct* testimony to its truth.

There is, however, a point which needs mentioning before we leave this part of the subject. Sometimes the best evidence for a miracle is not direct testimony, but indirect testimony. Let me explain. Direct testimony to an event X is a statement by some person or persons that they observed X. Indirect testimony to X is a statement by some person or persons that they observed something other than X (say Y), which is judged to be such that it could not have been observed unless X actually took place. This indirect testimony to an alleged miracle *has* a special weakness, and *seems* to have two special sources of strength. Of the latter, one is real and the other illusory. The evidence for X, based on indirect testimony, must have any weakness that the evidence for Y has, and it will have the additional weakness that the hypothesis that X actually happened may not be the only or the best explanation of the fact that Y was observed, even if the latter be true. On the other hand, Y may be quite a commonplace event, whilst X is a very extraordinary one. This does actually strengthen indirect testimony for X through Y, as against direct testimony for X, because the testimony for Y will not be vitiated by such factors as love of the wonderful, religious enthusiasm, etc., which tend to cast suspicion on the direct testimony for X. It also *seems* to strengthen the indirect testimony for X through Y, as against the direct testimony for X, because the intrinsic probability of Y will be much greater than that of X. But, in the long run, it does not do so. The testimony to Y only supports X in so far as the occurrence of X is the hypothesis that best explains the occurrence of Y. But the credibility of an hypothesis depends not merely on its ability to explain admitted facts, but also on its intrinsic probability. Thus the intrinsic improbability of X is as relevant to attempts to establish X through indirect testimony as to attempts to establish it through direct testimony. Still, on balance, a story of a miraculous event may be rendered much more probable by indirect than by direct testimony.

An example is provided by the story of the Resurrection in the Christian religion. The direct testimony for this event appears to me to be very feeble. It would be absurd, surely, to say that we have as good direct evidence for it as for the false story of the 80,000 Russians. But the indirect evidence is much stronger.[1] We have testimony to the effect that the disciples were exceedingly depressed at the time of the Crucifixion; that they had extremely little faith in the future; and that, after a certain time, this depression disappeared, and they believed that they had evidence that their Master had risen from the dead. Now none of these alleged facts is in the least odd or improbable, and we have therefore little ground for not accepting them on the testimony offered us. But having done this, we are faced with the problem of accounting for the facts which we have accepted. What caused the

---

[1] These points are excellently brought out in Samuel Butler's *Fair Haven*.

disciples to believe, contrary to their previous conviction, and in spite of their feeling of depression, that Christ had risen from the dead? Clearly, one explanation is that he actually had risen. And this explanation accounts for the facts so well that we may at least say that the indirect evidence for the miracle is far and away stronger than the direct evidence.

On the other hand, it does not seem to me that even the indirect evidence is strong in such a case. Such strength as it has springs from two roots: (*a*) The explanation does account for the facts which we have accepted on testimony; (*b*) No other explanation that has been put forward can be said to account equally well for them. But against this it must be said (*a*) that the miraculous explanation is intrinsically the least probable that can be put forward; and (*b*) that, in the present case, the failure of alternative explanations does not just leave the miraculous explanation standing alone; it leaves it with an indefinite number of other explanations which our lack of all detailed knowledge of the events immediately following the Crucifixion prevents us from formulating. We know that our state of ignorance is such that it is compatible with the existence of some quite simple explanation, and with the fact that no one will ever hit on this explanation.[2]

With these remarks we may leave Hume's special argument and pass to his general one.

§8. Hume's general argument against miracles seems to me to be weak in a number of ways. His definition of a miracle is very peculiar. He refuses to call an event a miracle unless it be the only event of the kind that has ever been known to happen. This is involved in his saying that a genuine miracle must contradict the *whole* course of experience. But surely there may be several events of the same kind which are all miracles, and all miraculous because of a single common circumstance. If Samuel was raised from the dead by the Witch of Endor, and if Lazarus was raised from the dead by Christ, these were both miracles. And they were both miracles of the same kind, *viz.*, contraventions of

---

[2] It is understood that the story of the 80,000 Russians originated through some third person reading a private telegram from a Russian to an English egg merchant. The words were, "80,000 Russians are coming"; and they referred to eggs, not to soldiers. A future historian, trying to account for the strange belief current in England in 1914, would hardly think of this explanation; and, if he put it forward as a conjecture, it would appear wild as compared with the hypothesis that the Russians actually did pass through England. There may be some equally simple explanation of the stories about the Resurrection; the true explanation may even have been hit upon by some sceptical biblical critic, and yet have been rejected by himself and others as too absurdly inadequate to account for the facts.

the natural law that when once a man dies he remains dead. It seems as if Hume would have to say that, if anybody has ever been raised from the dead, it was a miracle on the first occasion, because it contradicted all previous experience; but that, if it ever happened again, the second case would not be a miracle, because it did not contradict *all* previous experience. And then, I suppose, he would have to go back to the first case and deny that even this was really a miracle, because he would now say that it is not a genuine law of nature that people never come to life again after they are dead. I suppose that Hume's position really is that all miracles are solitary exceptions to some law of nature; but that you can never be sure that a solitary exception to some alleged law of nature is a miracle, because another exception may arise, and this will prove that we were not really concerned with a law of nature at all. This is not a satisfactory definition of a miracle. (*a*) It is, as we have seen, incompatible with the common view that miracles of the same kind may recur and be none the less miracles. (*b*) Unless miracles are to be ruled out as contradictions in terms—in which case the rest of Hume's arguments would be pointless—he must admit that a regularity does not cease to be a law of nature through a single alleged exception. But, if so, it seems arbitrary to suppose that two or three exceptions to a regularity necessarily prove that it is not a law of nature, and consequently that none of the exceptions are miraculous. (*c*) If this be granted, the important part of Hume's definition of a miracle will be that the event is caused by a particular volition of the Deity or by the interposition of some invisible agent; and this part of the definition is ignored in his subsequent argument.

§9. If we take Hume's argument seriously we get into difficulties over cases where no one supposes that there is a miracle. Clearly, many propositions have been accounted laws of nature because of an invariable experience in their favour, then exceptions have been observed, and finally these propositions have ceased to be regarded as laws of nature. But the first reported exception was, to anyone who had not himself observed it, in precisely the same position as a story of a miracle, if Hume be right. Those, then, to whom the first exception was reported ought to have rejected it, and gone on believing in the alleged law of nature. Yet, if the report of the first exception makes *no* difference to their belief in the law, their state of belief will be precisely the same when a second exception is reported as it was on the first occasion. Hence, if the first report ought to make no difference to their belief in the law, neither ought the second. So that it would seem on Hume's theory that if, up to a certain time, I and everyone else have always observed A to be followed by B, then no amount of testimony from the most trustworthy persons that they have observed A not followed by B ought to have the least effect on my belief in the law.

It might, of course, be said that I could examine the alleged exceptions for myself or explain them by other natural laws, and that then I ought to believe them. But the point is that if I acted as Hume seems to think I ought to act I should have no motive for doing either. My only motive for investigating alleged exceptions or trying to explain them is that the report of them has made me doubtful of the law. Yet, if the testimony of others does not shake my belief in the law, there is no reason for me to think that there is anything that needs explanation or investigation. If scientists had actually proceeded in this way, some of the most important natural laws would never have been discovered. For the people who discover exceptions to alleged general laws are seldom the same people who explain them. The former are often mere experimentalists and the latter mere mathematicians. Hence, if Hume were right, the people who could see that these were exceptions could not explain them; and the people who could explain them could not be persuaded that they exist.

Perhaps it will be contended that I am unfair to Hume here. It may be urged that, on his theory, my belief in a law, even when one exception only has been reported, cannot be precisely the same as it was before. It may be said that all that he means is that one reported exception, however well attested, ought never to reduce my belief in the laws so far as to change it to doubt or disbelief, though it must reduce my belief to some extent. This does seem to me to be the natural consequence of Hume's theory of belief and probability. But what follows? If one reported exception does reduce my belief in the law to some extent, how can we be sure that it will never reduce it from belief to doubt or disbelief? Hume's reply is that this is because we have only testimony, which, at its best, is not invariably trustworthy, to put against an experience which has *ex hypothesi* been so far uniform. But now suppose that a second exception is reported to me. My own experience in favour of the law is still uniformly favourable; my knowledge that the best human testimony is not invariably trustworthy has undergone no change. Why, then, should my belief in the law be further reduced by the testimony to the second exception than it was by the testimony to the first? If my own experience in favour of the law and my own experience of the general characteristics of human testimony be, as Hume seems to suggest, the only operative factors, the same startling results follow from the present milder interpretation of Hume's theory as from the earlier and more rigid one. If, on the other hand, concurrent testimony to *two* similar events may reduce my belief in a law to doubt or disbelief, in spite of my uniform experience in its favour, how can I possibly be sure that *no* amount of testimony to *one* such event can possibly reduce my belief so far? And, if I cannot be sure of this, how can I lay down the principle that *no* amount of testimony is sufficient to establish a miracle in Hume's sense of the word?

§10. Hume does not seem to notice that our belief in many natural laws rests mainly on testimony. There are many natural laws in which we all believe, but of which most of us have observed very few instances. *E.g.*, our belief that we shall die rests largely on testimony; most of us have met with very few cases of death in our own experience. So the evidence for and against an alleged miracle is mainly a matter of testimony against testimony. Nobody, *e.g.*, has had enough personal experience of death to make it reasonable for him to judge, simply from the regularity of his own experience, that a dead man never rises again. Our strong belief on this point is almost wholly due to the practically uniform testimony of other people. But we also know that there are a few accounts of men being raised from the dead. The position, therefore, is this. There is an enormous amount of testimony in favour of the view that all men once dead remain dead. There is a very little testimony in favour of the view that some dead men have risen again.

Let us suppose, for the sake of argument, that the testimony on one side seems as trustworthy as that on the other, and that the only difference is the amount of it on each side. Then we could interpret the fact in two ways. We might say: (*a*) It is not an absolutely general law of nature that all men once dead remain dead. Or we might say: (*b*) It is a general law of nature that all men once dead remain dead; but, in a few cases, this law has been contravened by a miracle. What would be the precise difference between these two interpretations of the facts?

§11. If we examined all the cases where people did come to life again and found that they had something common and peculiar to them, we need not suppose a miracle. Let the common quality be *q*. Then we should merely have to modify our general law and say: All men, except those who have the quality *q*, remain dead when they are once dead. This law would have no exceptions. And the resurrection of the persons with the quality *q* would not be a miracle, but merely an instance of another general law, *viz.*: All men who have the quality *q* can be raised from the dead.

It must be noticed that some explanation of this kind is always theoretically possible. It is therefore true to say that no testimony, however good, will *necessitate* a belief in a miracle. It is always possible (and nearly always reasonable), even if the alleged exceptional cases be admitted, to hold that they have some common and peculiar characteristic, though this may be too minute or obscure for us to detect.

§12. The other interpretation of the facts comes to this. The amount of testimony in favour of the law is so great that it seems reasonable to go on believing that the law is general. The exceptional cases have no common and peculiar quality that I can observe. If I conclude that they *really* have none, and wish to keep my belief in the law, I must suppose that the exceptions are due to the occasional interference of some supernatural force with nature. This practically means some agent acting upon matter or mind in the same direct way as that in which our minds apparently act on themselves and on our own bodies. It is not necessary to assume that this force obeys no laws; we should still call events due to the direct volitions of God, or an angel or devil or magician, miracles, even if we knew that these volitions obeyed among themselves psychological laws. To say that a law of nature is true, but that there are miraculous exceptions to it, comes, therefore, to this: the law is true independently of all conditions in the material world, but it may be suspended by something acting upon matter or other minds in the same direct way as our minds seem to act on our bodies and on themselves.

The notion of a miracle belongs mainly to popular thought. We cannot, therefore, expect to give a perfectly satisfactory definition of it. What seems clear is: (*a*) That the mere rarity of an event is not enough to make it count as a miracle; though, on the other hand, extreme frequency would probably hinder any event from being called miraculous. (*b*) If the instances of the event have something common and peculiar to them, more especially if this be a material quality, the events will not be called miracles. (*c*) The epithet "miraculous" involves a special interpretation of the causation of an event which *need* never be assumed. But, when it is assumed, it always seems to contain a reference to the direct action of a mind on other minds or on foreign matter. I think we may fairly say then that we have no sufficient evidence for supposing that a miracle has ever been performed in the course of history; but, at the same time, we have no sufficient evidence for saying that miracles cannot happen. The trouble about miracles, as it seems to me, is not that no evidence *could* prove one, but that no evidence *has* proved one.

§13. It remains to say something as to the consistency of Hume's theory about miracles with his own views about belief and causation. Hume has told us that he can find no logical ground for induction. He cannot see why it should be justifiable to pass from a frequent experience of A followed by B, to a belief that A always will be followed by B. All that he professes to do is to tell us that we actually do make this transition and to explain psychologically how it comes about. Now, this being so, I cannot see how Hume can distinguish between our variously caused beliefs about matters of fact, and call some of them justifiable and others unjustifiable.

Hume refuses to believe in a reported miracle, because it contradicts a constant experience of A followed by B, which has led to a strong belief that A always will be followed by B. A religious enthusiast believes a miracle because of a natural tendency to believe what is wonderful and what makes for the credit of his religion. In each case, we know the psychological cause of the belief. Hume's disbelief is due to his natural tendency to pass from the constant experience of A followed by B to the belief that A will always be followed by B. The enthusiast's belief is due to his natural tendency to believe what is wonderful and what makes for the credit of his religion. But Hume has admitted that he sees no logical justification for beliefs in matters of fact which are merely caused by a regular experience. Hence the enthusiast's belief in miracles and Hume's belief in natural laws (and consequent disbelief in miracles) stand on precisely the same logical footing. In both cases we can see the psychological cause of the belief, but in neither can Hume give us any logical ground for it.

We see, then, that Hume is really inconsistent in preferring a belief in the laws of nature based on constant experience to a belief in miracles based on the love of the wonderful. The inconsistency slips in when Hume says, not merely that we *do* tend to believe propositions with a strength proportional to the amount of experience and testimony in favour of them, but also that we *ought* to proportion our belief in this way. The first part of his statement is refuted by the case of the enthusiast, the second is rendered useless for him by his own sceptical theory of induction. On his own theories, he has no right to talk about what we *ought* to believe as to matters of fact. For what we ought to believe means what we are logically justified in believing, and Hume has said that he can find no logical justification for beliefs about matters of fact.

Probably the cause of this inconsistency in Hume was somewhat as follows: He seems to have thought that, as a matter of fact, there is some kind of harmony between our minds and the course of nature, so that, when a constant conjunction of A and B in our experience leads us to believe in a law connecting A and B in nature, this belief is actually quite often true, though we cannot give any logical justification for it. On the other hand, Hume, like everyone else, knew that beliefs which are caused merely by prejudice, or enthusiasm, or love of the wonderful, are as often false as true. So probably he would have stated his position somewhat as follows: I cannot pretend to offer any logical justification for your belief that A will always be followed by B, which is caused by your constant experience of A followed by B; but, all the same, we do seem to be so far in harmony with nature that beliefs caused in this way have, up to the present, turned out to be much oftener right than wrong. But beliefs caused by mere prejudice, or enthusiasm, or love of the wonderful, have, even up to the present, turned out to be much oftener wrong than right. So, a wise man will believe that A will be followed by B with a strength proportional to the regularity of his experience of A followed by B, and will not let himself attach much weight to alleged exceptions which flatter his love of the wonderful or his religious enthusiasm. It is true that he cannot give satisfactory logical grounds for his belief that A will always be followed by B; but he can give reasons for doubting alleged exceptions, since he knows that religious enthusiasm and love of the wonderful have no tendency to lead to true belief about matters of fact, and have often led to false ones. Indeed, whilst we cannot see why any of the causes that lead to our belief about matters of fact should lead to true belief, we can see that all such causes, except the regularity of our past experiences, have a strong tendency to lead to false ones.

Such a position is, I think, self-consistent. The only thing to be said is that it ought not to lead us to such a strong belief in any of the alleged laws of nature as to make us at once reject an alleged exception, no matter how good the testimony for it may be. We ought to be very slow indeed in admitting an alleged exception to a well-established law; and it may well be that there never has been good enough evidence for a reasonable man to accept any alleged miracle. But we have no right to say off-hand with Hume that no possible evidence *could* make it reasonable to suppose that a miraculous exception to some law of nature had taken place; and Hume, with his views of induction, has less right to say this than do most people.

HUME ON PERSONAL IDENTITY*[1]

Terence Penelhum

I want in this paper to examine the arguments which Hume uses in the famous Sixth Section of Part IV of Book I of the *Treatise*, not primarily as a work of scholarship, but in order to assess how good they are and to try to learn something from them when they are mistaken as well as when they are right. Hume's discussion of personal identity is the best there is; no one can feel the same about the problem after reading it as he did before; and, like so much that Hume says, it is incisive, penetrating, and most unsatisfying. It also has an additional, topical, interest: it gives us, I think, an excellent example of how complex and far-reaching the consequences of a mistake in linguistic or conceptual investigation can be.

I

To consider first the general problem with which Hume deals: the problem of personal identity can be roughly described as that of trying to justify a practice which seems at first sight to be strange, and even paradoxical. This is the practice of talking about people as single beings in spite of the fact that they are constantly changing, and over a period of time may have changed completely. It almost seems a contradiction to say that John Smith at two and John Smith at fifty-two are the same person, because they are so different.

* From *The Philosophical Review*, LXIV (1955), 571–589. Reprinted by permission of the author and *The Philosophical Review*.
[1] This paper is a revised version of one read to a meeting of the Pacific Division of the American Philosophical Association at the University of Washington, Seattle, on September 8, 1954, and was published the following year. While I think the general lines of criticism adopted here are still sound, and have therefore attempted no further revisions, it is obvious that anyone writing on these themes now would have to take account of recent work on self-identity, especially that of P. F. Strawson in *Individuals* and Sydney Shoemaker in *Self-Knowledge and Self-Identity*. In particular, this would make what I say in section III and in section VI (1) better than it is as it stands. I have tried to take some account of the aspects of Hume's problem that this paper overlooks in my article "Personal Identity," to appear in the forthcoming Crowell-Collier *Encyclopedia of Philosophy*, edited by Paul Edwards.

Of course the same problem could be raised in the case of other things—think of Heraclitus and the river. It might look as though the problem of personal identity were just one case of a general problem of the persistence of an object through change, and that any special interest we had in personal identity, rather than in fluminal, floral, or faunal identity, arose from the fact that the kind of thing in question is nearer home. But this last fact has had other effects as well: we are in a position to know that human beings have feelings and thoughts and images and pains, and that although these can be talked about by others, they cannot be *seen* or *had* by them, even though our bodily movements are open to public inspection. Now there has been a tendency among philosophers to do more than just recognize that people's lives *include* such private happenings—the tendency has been to regard them as forming a separate *thing* which has a purely contingent relationship to the body. This tendency to dualism has frequently restricted the way in which the problem of personal identity has been put. It has ceased to be "How are we to account for the unity we assume people to have throughout their lives?" and has become "How are we to account for the unity possessed by one *mind* throughout the changes in its (uniformly private) states?" A result of this restriction has been the invention of an entity called "the self," which Hume very properly derides. The purpose its invention serves is this: There is a certain type of solution to the problem of the identity of changing things which consists in saying that in spite of all appearances, which it is admitted are certainly to the contrary, there in fact *is* some item in the composition of changing objects, which does *not* change in any respect. A partiality to this type of solution in the case of persons might quite naturally lead to making the unchanging item a private one; but if this partiality is combined with the dualistic view of the nature of persons, then it is inevitable that the seat of personal identity should be thought to lie in the mind, and the unchanging item be mental. This is, of course, "the self," which Hume begins by attacking. I shall now turn to his actual argument,[2] and expound it briefly.

II

He has already maintained in the previous Section that no one has rendered intelligible the relationship of "support" which is supposed to

---

[2] All quotations in what follows are taken from the Selby-Bigge edition of Hume's *Treatise*, published at Oxford by the Clarendon Press. I have only given page references in the case of moderately lengthy quotations.

hold between "the self" and the other components of our mental histories. In Section VI he opens by disposing of the view that the existence of the self can be recognised empirically—he does this very simply by denying that anyone can find it, unless, of course, its defenders are differently constituted from himself. Assuming that this is not the case, then the whole of mankind are "nothing but a bundle or collection of different perceptions" in a constant state of change. There is none of the simplicity or identity that the self was supposed to provide. This means that it is a mistake to "suppose ourselves possessed of an invariable and uninterrupted existence through the whole course of our lives." Yet we all do suppose it (not merely, Hume implies, the philosophers who try to justify us). How does this mistake arise?

It is based, Hume says, on the confusion between two ideas: (a) that of an object which persists throughout a length of time without change or interruption—this is the idea of identity; (b) that of a succession of related objects—this, he says, is clearly a case of diversity.

We confuse these two because the succession is a succession of *related* objects, and contemplating or imagining such a succession feels much the same as contemplating or imagining an unchanging and uninterrupted object. Having been thus confused, we "substitute" the idea of identity for that of a related succession. And we cannot free ourselves from this confusion for long; the only result of reflecting on it is the bogus attempt to justify it by inventing "some new and unintelligible principle," like "substance" or "the self," which is somehow supposed to preserve the sequence unchanged.

To prove this thesis Hume thinks he has merely to show that those things we (mistakenly) call the same even though they are changing and interrupted consist of a succession of related parts. To show this he takes various kinds of changing things, claiming in each case that the relation of the change to the whole which changes causes us to overlook its occurrence and continue to call the object the same. (The change, for example, is small in proportion to the whole, takes place only gradually, leaves the function of the whole unaffected, etc.) The same principles are at work in the case of persons; so in their case, as in all other cases, the identity we ascribe to them is "fictitious."

Hume ends by saying that his whole examination of this question reveals that most of the disputes about identity are "merely verbal." Since, as he puts it, "identity depends on the relations of ideas, and these relations produce identity by means of that easy transition they occasion," when these relations and the ease of transition grow less, the tendency to believe in identity grows less too. He gives no example here, but the kind of thing I take it he has in mind is this (I shall take a simple and nonpersonal instance): If a philosopher were to take a particular case like the history of a building from its initial construction to its final demolition, and were to ask at what point what was originally a mere pile of bricks became the house, and at what point what had been the house ceased to be this and gave place to a mere pile of bricks once more (should we date these events by the laying or crumbling of the foundations, or the tiling or stripping of the roof, or the installation or removal of the plumbing? etc., etc.), the answer to give him would be that the tendency to ascribe identity to the changing and complex object is in this case based on the relationship which all the parts have to a central function, viz., the usefulness of the building for sheltering people, but that when this relationship is equivocal (e.g., when the structure could hold people, but only uncomfortably) we simply have a stretch of time when the tendency to say that this is a house rather than a heap of bricks exists, but with less force. At such a time we can decide much as we please which to say it is, and it does not really matter. Our decision would only matter if we invented some philosophical fiction to bolster it up.

III

I wish first to comment briefly on Hume's statement that the whole of mankind are "nothing but a bundle or collection of different perceptions." What is meant by this? Part of what he means is, of course, that human beings are not composed of something called a "self" *plus* some other, less permanent, items, but only of these latter items themselves. So much would be a mere reiteration of what he has already said. But he is clearly committing himself besides to something much stronger and stranger than this, viz., to the view that these items of which, and of nothing-else-but, the whole of mankind are composed are "perceptions." Now this claim is clearly not of quite the same sort as the claim of some philosophers that material things are nothing but perceptions. For, (a) this latter claim is usually somewhat to the effect that statements made about any material thing can somehow be construed as being in fact statements about some of the things that happen to observers when they look at it; and if this were the sort of thing that Hume meant by saying that *people* were nothing but perceptions, it would follow that according to him each person is composed of *other people's* perceptions, that every statement about a given person ought to be construed as a statement about some *other* person or persons; I feel confident that he does not mean this. (b) I feel confident also that he is using the word "perception" in a much wider sense than the sense in which it is used by philosophers who claim that material things are nothing but perceptions, since they use it to mean events which might otherwise be called "sensations," whereas he seems to include in its meaning such events as dreams, feelings, images, etc.—all those events I mentioned earlier which are not open to public view in the way in which our bodily movements are.

What Hume's claim about human beings involves, then, is that they are nothing but the series of *their own* sensations, feelings, dreams, images, and the rest. Clearly, to reach this conclusion he must have been dealing not with the question "How are we justified in attributing identity to persons?" but the question "How are we justified in attributing identity to *minds?*" (where the word "mind" is understood as meaning the "theatre," to use Hume's own term, where these private events take place). It is far from trivial to notice that these two questions are not equivalent (obviously not, since the words "person" and "mind" are not); for answering the latter rather than the former restricts the discussion of personal identity considerably. It forces us to ignore, for example, that the most common way of settling practical problems of identification is by scrutinizing people's physical appearance; or that the gradualness of the changes in complex things which Hume claims to be one of the main contributing causes of our calling them identical is only a feature of human beings if one thinks of them partly in terms of their physical careers; or that the uninterruptedness which he thinks we erroneously attribute to them is in fact a feature of their physical lives.

Fortunately, however, this restriction does not affect the pertinence of his discussion as much as it might be expected to do. This is due to the fact that although he talks at various points as though the problem he is trying to answer is that of the unity of the *mind*, and refers to that of personal identity as though it were the same, the way in which he tries to illumine it is by putting forward a *general* thesis, which I have already outlined, concerning the *general* propensity to call complex and changing objects identical, a propensity of which the ascription of identity to persons is just one instance. It follows, therefore, that the objections I have just raised would apply rather to his view of what sort of thing a person *is* than to his *general* view of the *kinds* of factor at work when we ascribe identity to changing and complex things, whether they are persons or not. I am prepared to agree with him (a) that persons are changing and complex, and (b) that such features as the proportionate smallness of changes, or their gradualness,

which he says consolidate our propensity, can be found in the case of
persons (more easily, in fact, if we recognize that "person" means more
than just "mind"), and this is all that it is necessary to agree to in order
to admit that his thesis applies to the case of persons. My subsequent
comments will be concerned with this central and general thesis, and
are therefore independent of the foregoing criticisms of Hume's view
that the life-histories of persons have merely mental components, just
as the thesis itself could be stated independently of this view.

IV

Hume's thesis turns on one central point, and stands or falls with
it. This point is his contention that it is, "to a more accurate method of
thinking," a confusion to call an object that changes the *same*. The
"idea of identity or sameness" is the idea of an object that persists *without* changing. The fact that the parts of a changing thing may be related to one another does not, after all, alter the further fact that they
do change; so in this case we do *not* have identity or sameness, and it
must therefore be due to some ingrained tendency of the mind that we
talk as though we do. From this point, which he brings in fairly un-
obtrusively, the remainder of his arguments follow naturally:

(1) The puzzle that remains is a psychological one, viz., what is
it about us that makes this mistake possible?

(2) Any account of the relationships that hold between the parts
of complex things will only be relevant to *this* question; they do not
affect the question of whether we are *justified* in calling such objects
the same, because we just aren't.

(3) Clearly, the borderline cases, where we are undecided
whether to say that what is before us is the same object or another one,
as it were, taking over where the first one left off, are merely verbal
and undecidable because *whatever* we decide will be groundless and
mistaken. For the very fact that a change is taking place ought strictly
to make us say it is not the same object, but the fact that other changes
have preceded this one should have made us say that long before. There
is no difference in *kind* between the borderline cases and the times of
change during the previous history of the object. The only difference is
in the degree of psychological compulsion acting on us—the propensity
to misapply the notion of identity is beginning to falter when the
borderline is reached, but has not done so before. The only possible
standard is violated at *all* stages.

(4) The fictions of the self and substance have arisen because philosophers have sensed the nature of our common mistake, but have not

been able to free themselves from it for long. The inevitable result of this conflict-state is that they have felt there *must*, really, underneath, out of sight, be an unchanging something-or-other which is the real object, so that our strange habit is justified after all.

All of these are natural consequences of what Hume says about the nature of identity in the early part of the Section. If it is true that we make a mistake in the first place by talking of identity through change at all, then all the rest follows. But I think it is not hard to show that *he* is making an elementary error here, not everyone else, and that the facts he brings to our notice are twisted and misapplied as a result.

It is important to keep in mind as one reads him that he does think he has uncovered a *mistake*, as his language does not always lay stress on this. For instance, when talking about persons, he says:

I cannot compare the soul more properly than to a republic or common-wealth . . . as the same individual republic may not only change its members, but also its laws and constitutions; in like manner the same person may vary his character and disposition, as well as his impressions and ideas, without losing his identity.[3]

This does not, taken out of context, sound like the account of an alleged mistake at all, but it is quite clear from everything that has led up to it that it is, including in particular the fact that this passage is intended as a demonstration that the identity of the mind of a person is a "fictitious" one. The same applies too, of course, to the identity of a republic or commonwealth. Hume is not just saying that our common practice of attributing identity in such cases cannot be justified, or has no sound reason in its favor (as he says of our belief in the regularity of nature): he is here making the less modest claim that our common practice is wrong, that the evidence points unequivocally to the opposite. We proceed not without, but in the face of, the evidence. But it would seem from the tone of the above passage, as well as from his well-known second thoughts in the Appendix, that even Hume found this odd and paradoxical sometimes.

For odd and paradoxical it certainly is. What he is actually claiming is that we are constantly making a mistake in referring to a person from day to day as the same person (in using the same proper name, for example), or in referring in this way to *anything* that has changed in the slightest. For, strictly speaking, a changed person would be literally *another* person. A little effort of imagination is enough to indicate just how much chaos would result from adopting Hume's diagnosis as the

[3] *Treatise*, p. 261.

source of a prescription and using a different proper name whenever
we noticed the slightest change, even in ourselves (or rather in the
separate people that we would be from minute to minute). If we make
a *mistake* in *not* doing this, it is a mistake we *all* make *all* the time, and
a mistake of which the correction would require a complete overhaul of
the concepts and syntax of our language. I suppose Hume would say
this is one of the reasons why we continue to make the mistake—to
avoid the desperate awkwardness of trying to live up to our moments
of philosophical insight all the time. But I find it hard to believe that
a mistake lies at the root of so much of our language, especially since
Hume has claimed to reveal it by a piece of linguistic analysis. I want
to show that his analysis is a bad one, that the "mistake" is not a mistake
at all, and that its supposed revelation is not a piece of philosophical insight, but of short sight, or rather, astigmatism.

Once the basic point is located, it is not hard to see that Hume
has gone wrong. Let us consider the essential three sentences:

We have a distinct idea of an object, that remains invariable and uninterrupted thro' a suppos'd variation of time; and this idea we call that of
identity or *sameness*. We have also a distinct idea of several different objects
existing in succession, and connected together by a close relation; and this
to an accurate view affords as perfect a notion of *diversity*, as if there was
no manner of relation among the objects. But tho' these two ideas of
identity, and a succession of related objects be in themselves perfectly distinct, and even contrary, yet 'tis certain, that in our common way of thinking, they are generally confounded with each other.[4]

It is not hard to find his error here. What he is saying is that since we
would call something the same for a given length of time when it con-
tinued without any alteration, and since we would say that a succession
of objects was a collection or number or series of objects, it would
obviously be a contradiction to say that in the latter case we would have
one object. In a sense this is true, but not in the sense which Hume requires. He has not noticed what is wrong because he has chosen to talk
in very general terms here, and to ignore the way in which we would
actually talk on particular occasions. But a rebuttal can be produced
even in general terms. Let us call the unchanging single object X. X, we
would say, is the same throughout. Let us call our succession of distinct
but related objects *A, B, C, D, E, F*, etc. Here, if we count, we obviously have several, not one. But we can quite easily produce a class-
name for the series of them, say φ, such that a φ is, by definition, any
group of things like *A, B, C, D, E, F*, etc. So there would be no con-

[4] *Ibid.*, p. 253.

tradiction in saying there are six objects and one φ; this is what a φ *is*. Quite obviously, our ordinary language works this way. A succession of notes is one theme. A succession of words is one sentence. If the succession does not form a theme or sentence, it is still a *succession* or series. There is no contradiction in saying "There are six notes in this theme," or "There are six words in this sentence," though there would be in saying "There are six notes but only one," or "There are six words but only one." Naturally, *this* would be absurd, but no one ever says it (for that reason).

So, in spite of Hume, there is no contradiction in saying that certain kinds of things are composed of a succession of parts, and yet are each only one thing. Whether a thing can have many parts or not depends entirely on what sort of thing it is. Most things (including people) do.

There is another, closely related, mistake which Hume has made. This is the mistake of thinking that for anything to be entitled to be called "the same" it has to remain *unchanged* from one period to the next. This is a muddle of two things that he himself distinguishes at one point, viz., the two distinct senses of the word "identical" or "the same." These are the numerical and the specific senses, as he calls them. Two things can be the same as one another in the specific sense, i.e., exactly alike in some respect, yet they will still be two things; but if they are said to be the same in the numerical sense, they are being said to be not two things but one, after all. These two senses are distinct from one another. Now, to remain unchanged is to remain the same in the *specific* sense, i.e., to be now exactly as one was at an earlier time. But I can remain the same in the *numerical* sense without doing so in the specific sense—I can be numerically the same but changed. In fact, I cannot be said to have changed unless I *am* the same in the numerical sense. The only reason for saying that something is numerically different (something else, that is) when a change occurs, is if it is by definition an unchanging thing. When a note is played, for example, as soon as the tone is raised or lowered we have another note, not the same one at all. But in the case of most things, the words we use to talk about them are words the meanings of which allow us or require us to continue to use them throughout certain changes, though not, of course, *any* changes. What kind of changes can occur without our having to say that the thing has ceased to exist and given place to something else depends on what *kind* of thing we are talking about. To know what such changes are is part of what it is to know the meaning of the class-term for that sort of object. A house, or a person, is something which admits of many changes before we would say it had ceased to exist. To know what these changes are is to know, in part at least, what the words "house" and "person" mean.

The rejoinder to Hume, then, consists simply in saying that the pairs of expressions, (a) "numerically the same" and "containing many parts" and (b) "numerically the same" and "changed," are not pairs of contradictories. So we have not made a mistake in saying that a succession of related objects may form a unit of a certain kind, or that the same thing may undergo radical changes. Once this is admitted, the rest of what he says appears in quite a different light.

V

(1) His *examples* point quite a different moral from what he thinks:

(a) The paragraph I quoted can hardly be said to contain an example, but if we produce examples to fit it we get quite different results from those Hume intended. There is nothing about "an object that remains invariable and uninterrupted" *per se* which requires us to say it is the same thing throughout, and nothing about a succession of different but related ones *per se* which requires the opposite. It depends entirely on what concepts we are using when we talk about each. If we heard a continuous sound we would say it was one sound and not several; but it is not hard to imagine some situation in which we would be interested in counting the number of seconds of sound, in which case we would say there were, for example, ten of them. In the case of a succession of objects, the whole series might very well be said to form a unit: a succession of men may form a march-past. There is nothing revealing in choosing a single and uninterrupted sort of thing rather than a complex thing, and Hume has fallen into a conceptual muddle by doing so. He only makes it worse by talking of "an *object* that remains invariable" and "several *objects* existing in succession," because he is here using the same noun in each case, viz., "object"; and although this is the vaguest noun in the language, the mere fact that he uses the same one in each case suggests very easily that in the two phrases he is thinking of objects of the same kind, e.g., a single and uninterrupted note and a succession of distinct notes. This would point a contrast, though of dubious value to Hume;[5] but if we took the

---

[5] It would be of dubious value to him because although if we replaced "object" by the same noun in each phrase we would get a contrast, we would quite clearly get a case where the confusion he has in mind would be altogether unlikely.

variable-word "object" at its face value and substituted different nouns in each phrase, the contrast would disappear: where is there a contrast between "an invariable and uninterrupted arithmetical progression" and "a succession of different but related numbers"? If it is thought that I have chosen a favorable example here, the reply is that I am quite entitled to do so. I am quite ready to admit that we could find a contrast here by making different substitutions, but this just bears out the essential point that whether we get one or not depends entirely on what nouns we choose to work with, and not on the concepts of identity and diversity. Put generally, whether the result is logically absurd, or logically possible, or logically necessary, if the two phrases "the same continuing x" and "several different y's" are used of the same thing, depends entirely on what nouns we use to replace x and y. It does not depend on the words "same" and "different" in themselves.

(b) There are two specific examples which Hume does offer, but misunderstands. He offers both as instances of confusion between numerical and specific identity. The first is this:

A man, who hears a noise, that is frequently interrupted and renew'd, says it is still the same noise; tho' 'tis evident the sounds have only a specific identity or resemblance, and there is nothing numerically the same, but the cause, which produc'd them.[6]

I do not think the man in this case would be guilty of this confusion. When he says it is still the same noise, he may mean one of two things: (i) he might be using "same" in the specific sense, in which case he would be saying merely that the noise he hears now is exactly like the one he heard before; or (ii) he might be using the word "noise" as roughly equivalent to "an intermittent series of exactly similar sounds," in which case the constituent sounds of the noise, in this sense of "noise," can certainly come and go.

The second example is this:

In like manner it may be said, without breach of the propriety of language, that such a church, which was formerly of brick, fell to ruin, and that the parish rebuilt the same church of free-stone, and according to modern architecture. Here neither the form nor materials are the same, nor is there anything common to the two objects, but their relation to the inhabitants of the parish; and yet this alone is sufficient to make us denominate them the same.[7]

Here again the example does not bear out Hume's views at all. Of *course* the relationship of the building to the inhabitants is enough for

[6] *Treatise*, p. 258.
[7] *Ibid.*, p. 258.

us to call it the same, because the concept with which we are operating, say that of "the village church of Muddlehampton" is simply and solely the concept of *any* structure which has the unique purpose at any period of subserving the religious needs of the people of that parish. This is why we would use the same phrase whatever building was there, and would say, both before and after the rebuilding, that we had the same thing there; for, in the sense of the concept we would be using, we *would* have the same thing there. There is no mistake in this, as there would be in saying we had the same building, in the sense of the same pile of stones; but we would not say *that*. The village church of Muddlehampton can be pulled down and rebuilt again many times over with perfect logical propriety.

(2) But Hume's error of supposing that invariance is the standard of identity in all cases, when it is only the standard in a very few (those in which invariance is part of the concept of the thing), makes him not only misunderstand the import of his own examples, but miss the point of his otherwise very revealing account of *the relations between the parts of complex things.* Factors like the proportionate smallness of changes, or the conspiracy of the remaining parts to the same end, he claims to be factors which make us overlook the fact that changes have occurred at all. But we do not overlook this fact; we are perfectly aware of it. What Hume is actually describing here in general terms are the kinds of changes that are comprehended under the concepts of certain sorts of things. It is true that these are often small in proportion to the whole, that they take place slowly, and so on. But it is not true always; it is not true of the concept of a river, as Hume himself says. It depends on the concept. As he puts it himself, "What is natural and essential to any thing is, in a manner, expected"; that is to say, more changes are allowed in some things than others, depending on the kind. He should have added, "and it is embodied in the concept of the thing." This might have stopped him saying that these natural and essential changes merely make us misapply the concept of identity, and revealed instead that the standards for applying the concept of identity depend entirely on the substantives it is joined onto. The rules for using nouns (and it is the *modus operandi* of nouns to which his description is relevant) are evolved by generations of language-users, and we have to decide in terms of these at what point a noun applies to whatever we may be considering and when it ceases to.

(3) This decision is not always easy, since the rules we apply are at best very general ones, learned from experience, and not able to cover every eventuality. There are inevitable times when we do not

know just what term applies. These are the *borderline cases*, the occasions when the "nice and subtle" questions about identity start coming up. In deciding whether the roofless structure in front of us is a house or a heap of stones, we may have reached a point where the conventions governing neither expression are sufficient to tell us, and we just have to decide for ourselves and, in so doing, make these conventions more precise. We can make mistakes here, like taking a decision which has unforeseen legal repercussions regarding the status of our property. But we do not make a mistake just because we are considering saying it is the same object when it has changed. Hume would have to say that in this case we are merely repeating an error which we have made many times already during the object's history, and just happen for strictly psychological reasons to be feeling uneasy about it this time. But we are uneasy because the rules for our words are not geared to meet every eventuality, not because they ought not to meet any at all. It is true that we lack a standard, but not because we have not been following one before.

(4) It is now time to consider *Hume's criticisms of other philosophers*. He pours scorn on theories of "the self" and "substance," whether they claim to be empirical or not. I do not want to dwell on his criticisms of these theories, since they seem to me to be sound ones. I am more interested in discussing his account of how such theories arise. He claims that they arise because philosophers, like the rest of us, are subject to those factors which produce the mistake of allowing numerical identity to complex and changing things, but are occasionally made aware, by the kind of argument he himself uses, that they *are* making this mistake. Being human, and unable therefore to shake off this pernicious but convenient confusion, they have eventually tried to justify it by inventing fictions like "the self" to meet the requirement of invariance that they see could not be met otherwise. I have suggested that the factors he has enumerated do not contribute to a mistake or confusion, because there is none. But I agree that the self is a fiction. Such fictions have quite probably arisen in the way Hume describes. That is, the philosophers in question may have thought they found a contradiction between saying a thing has changed and saying it is still the same thing; and they may have tried to overcome this by saying that there is in fact some crucial respect in which the thing will *not* have changed, and inventing the self to fill the bill. But if I am right, they need not have bothered; since there is no contradiction there to be avoided, the fiction is unnecessary. What is of more interest is that Hume, in exposing the nature of their mistake, has conceded their

main premise, viz., that there *is* a contradiction there, and has merely said that it is impossible to avoid it and recommended us by implication not to try to justify it. This is a sturdier course than theirs; but, as it proceeds from the same starting-point, it is not surprising that Hume's solution seems to him the sort of paradoxical scepticism for which the only cure is a change of subject or a game of backgammon. This is all the result, as far as I can see, of a linguistic error, of a misdescription of the way in which certain words in the language are in fact used.

I must now try to anticipate a criticism: it might seem that I have been too severe on Hume, too keen to stress the consequences of a position which is more austere than the one he actually holds. I might appear to have missed the point of the fact (noted above) that as his discussion proceeds he does not seem to be *objecting* to the practice of calling people, for all their complexity and changingness, the same throughout their lives; in the course of several pages devoted to the psychological influences on our linguistic conventions, Hume does not seem to be *criticizing*, but only to be *describing* the way in which we talk. He certainly says that our tendency to talk of changing things as identical is a mistake and a confusion, but he only says this at the beginning, in an attempt to discredit philosophical constructs like the self, which only occur when philosophers try to justify, or show rational ground for, a practice which is just a matter of habit and could not conceivably depend on anything *they* had to say. Hume is not trying to discredit our usage, but only to discredit misguided attempts to defend it.

This sort of view is held by Professor Kemp Smith,[8] who insists that Hume has no objection to our everyday use of the notion of identity, once this is understood to be based on custom and not on argument. It would follow from this (and Kemp Smith accepts this consequence) that when Hume refers to the identity of persons as "fictitious," he does not mean *fictitious*, but something less censorious, something more like "stretched": Kemp Smith suggests "Pickwickian." So, although he begins by maintaining that "to an accurate view" talk of the changing or complex as identical is paradoxical, Hume is not himself disposed to take the accurate view, nor to urge it on others—the fact that it is a universal custom *not* to take the accurate view makes it pointless to attempt to impose it in any case.

---

[8] N. K. Smith, *The Philosophy of David Hume* (New York, 1941). See particularly pp. 96–98, 497–505.

I have no particular wish either to welcome or to resist this interpretation of Hume's position, or to discuss how far Hume is consistent if this reading of his position is correct. For it is irrelevant to my main contentions:

(a) Whether he is saying that our habit of talking involves us in a paradox which we render tolerable by certain psychological mechanisms, or that the habit is only paradoxical when we take an over-scrupulous view of it, but justifies itself pragmatically somehow and should therefore not distress us, he is in either case saying that it can be shown to involve a paradox on examination. However lightly he takes it, he believes it is there. I have denied it is there at all, whether we take an "accurate view" or not.

(b) Whether he thinks the use of the word "identical" with reference to complex things or changing things is a mistaken use or merely a stretched use, he certainly thinks the word is being at least mildly abused on these occasions. I have denied this.

(c) Whether his account of what makes us talk of identity in this mistaken or Pickwickian way is intended as a description of how we hide the paradox from ourselves, or merely of what enables us to talk with a (perfectly proper) lack of concern for it, it is in either case misdirected, since our apparent unconcern for the paradox is due to its nonexistence, and what he in fact describes are the factors governing the use of substantives, and not the *mis*use of the adjective "same."

In other words, however tolerant of our linguistic behavior Hume may be, there is nothing for him to be tolerant about.

VI

Two points in conclusion: (1) I have not paid special attention to personal identity rather than any other kind. Here I am following Hume. While his chapter and my comments might well have been enriched by descriptions of the relationships between the various stages and facets of the life of persons, such descriptions would have been incidental to the issue which is the core of his argument, viz., the analysis of the concept of identity, and in particular its compatibility or incompatibility with the concepts of complexity and change. This question is the same whatever complex or changing objects we choose to take as examples. Admittedly, persons have a greater degree of complexity and a greater tendency to change than most other things, but to explore this complexity and these changes is to illuminate the concept of a person rather than that of identity.

But there is a positive danger also in laying special emphasis on persons, a danger to which Hume is very much alive: it makes one very susceptible to the suggestion that as we are persons ourselves we are in a better position in this one case to locate the unchanging particle which carries our identity with it, since we have access to human life from the inside as well as the outside. This makes it tempting to give a term like "the self" a quasi-empirical character, as though it referred to an object of introspection. It has been suggested that when this happens it is easy to believe that certain somatic sensations are revelations of the self. If this is true it might explain some of the (otherwise very extraordinary) empirical claims of the kind Hume mentions. It is one thing to claim the self must be there, but quite another to claim you have found it. But to follow the scent of this red herring is to be diverted from recognizing that the whole purpose for which the search was instigated is misconceived.

(2) Hume's language throughout makes it clear that he thinks the error he claims to detect is committed by everyone, that is, by every user of the language, not just by philosophers. If I am right, this is not the case and the ordinary language-user is quite innocent. He clearly holds that it is the philosophers who have invented the fictions of substances and selves. Here, he is right, of course. What emerges from this is that such philosophers, in inventing their fictions, are not defending the layman at all. For they concede, with Hume, that the only chance of showing there is no such paradoxical error in the layman's language is by finding the unchanging kernel within each changing thing. But the layman does not need this sort of defense, because there is no paradox there in the first place. So any claim that the doctrine of the self is a defense of the layman or that it represents the "common sense position," if this means the same, would be bogus. This point is in no way altered by the fact (and it does seem to be one) that laymen beginning philosophy tend to prefer substance-type theories. For this would be the result of unclear theorizing *about* language (quite a different activity from the mere using of language, and demanding quite distinct aptitudes—rather as travel and cartography differ). Someone new to linguistic theorizing could quite well think he detected a paradox where others claimed to, and fail to notice that his own daily practice did not bear this out. Once this happened, the self might very well seem the only way of evading the paradox. But at this point we are not dealing with a layman any more, but with a philosophical novice. A view which the plain-man-newly-turned-philosopher prefers is not necessarily one he is committed to beforehand.

Suggested Further Readings

PAPERBACK EDITIONS OF HUME'S "ENQUIRY"

David Hume, *An Enquiry Concerning Human Understanding* (La Salle, Ill.: Open Court Publishing Co., 1958). This edition contains several sections from the *Treatise,* including the section on personal identity.

———, *An Inquiry Concerning Human Understanding* (New York: Bobbs-Merrill Library of Liberal Arts, 1955).

———, *An Enquiry Concerning Human Understanding* (Chicago: Regnery, 1956).

———, *On Human Nature and the Understanding* (New York: Collier Books, 1962). This edition of the *Enquiry* includes a large number of sections from the *Treatise,* including the section on personal identity.

———, *Selections* (New York: Charles Scribner's Sons, 1927). This does not contain a complete edition of the *Enquiry,* but does include extensive selections from Hume's other writings, including his discussion of personal identity.

BOOKS ABOUT HUME

A. H. Basson, *David Hume* (Baltimore, 1958).
Antony Flew, *Hume's Philosophy of Belief* (New York, 1961).
C. W. H. Hendel, *Studies in the Philosophy of David Hume* (Princeton, 1925).
J. Laird, *Hume's Philosophy of Human Nature* (London, 1932).
D. G. C. MacNabb, *David Hume: His Theory of Knowledge and Morality* (London, 1951).
E. C. Mossner, *The Life of David Hume* (London, 1954).
D. F. Pears (ed.), *David Hume: A Symposium* (New York, 1963).
H. H. Price, *Hume's Theory of the External World* (Oxford, 1940).
N. Kemp Smith, *The Philosophy of David Hume* (London, 1949).

BOOKS CONTAINING CHAPTERS OR SECTIONS
DISCUSSING HUME

A. J. Ayer, *The Foundations of Empirical Knowledge* (London, 1947).
H. L. A. Hart and A. M. Honore, *Causation in the Law* (Oxford, 1959).

116 *Suggested Further Readings*

G. E. Moore, *Philosophical Studies* (London, 1922)
————, *Some Main Problems of Philosophy* (London, 1953).
H. A. Prichard, *Knowledge and Perception* (Oxford, 1950).
Karl R. Popper, *Conjectures and Refutations* (New York, 1962).
H. Reichenbach, *The Rise of Scientific Philosophy* (Berkeley, 1951).

ARTICLES

R. F. Atkinson, "Hume on Mathematics," *Philosophical Quarterly*, X (1960), 127–137.
P. Butcharov, "The Self and Perceptions," *Philosophical Quarterly*, IX (1959), 97–115.
M. F. Dummett, "Can an Effect Precede Its Cause?" *Proceedings of the Aristotelian Society*, Supp. vol. XXVIII (1954), 27–44.
B. M. Laing, "Hume's *Dialogues*," *Philosophy*, XII (1937), 175–190.
C. A. Mace, "Hume's Doctrine of Causality," *Proceedings of the Aristotelian Society*, XXIII (1931–1932), 301–328.
James Noxon, "Hume's Agnosticism," *Philosophical Review*, LXXIII (1964), 248–261.
Nelson Pike, "Hume on Evil," *Philosophical Review*, LXXII (1963), 180–197.
R. Popkin, "David Hume: His Pyrrhonism and His Critique of Pyrrhonism," *Philosophical Quarterly*, vol. I, 1950.
N. Kemp Smith, "David Hume," *Proceedings of the Aristotelian Society*, Supp. vol. XVIII (1939), i–xxxiv.
"Symposium on Self Identity," *Proceedings of the Aristotelian Society*, Supp. vol. XVIII (1939), 1–48.
John W. Yolton, "The Concept of Experience in Locke and Hume," *Journal of the History of Philosophy*, I (1963), 53–72.